MICHIBIKI
The Leading of God

Dr. Raymond S. Moore

Illustrations by Stanley Dunlap, Jr.

World rights reserved. This book or any portion thereof may not be copied or reproduced in any form or manner whatever, except as provided by law, without the written permission of the publisher, except by a reviewer who may quote brief passages in a review.

The author assumes full responsibility for the accuracy of all facts and quotations as cited in this book. The opinions expressed in this book are the author's personal views and interpretations, and do not necessarily reflect those of the publisher.

This book is provided with the understanding that the publisher is not engaged in giving spiritual, legal, medical, or other professional advice. If authoritative advice is needed, the reader should seek the counsel of a competent professional.

Copyright © 2023 Raymond and Dorothy Moore
Copyright © 2023 TEACH Services, Inc.
ISBN-13: 978-1-4796-1100-3 (Paperback)
ISBN-13: 978-1-4796-1101-0 (ePub)

Published by

www.TEACHServices.com • (800) 367-1844

Dedication

To the teachers and students of Japan Missionary College, whose earnestness, loyalty, and sweet Christian spirit were a constant inspiration.

Contents

Foreword vii

When Is a Call from God? 9

Prisoners' Food 17

The Coming of the Prince 23

The Providential Dr. Waterfield 31

Providence on the Campus 39

Winning the Mombusho 43

The Chosen Three 49

Yasushi and God 53

Paddies and Promises 61

The Gambler Takes a Chance 67

Two Wrongs Make It Right 73

Fumio San 79

God Turns the Battle 85

Adventures of a Scientist 93

Imamura's Blessings 101

The Makings of Heroes 109

Yamamoto Finds a Daniel 117

God and the Gyoraitei 125

From the Shadow of the Gallows to the Shadow of the Cross .. 133

Foreword

As day to day the hand of God was more and more clearly seen in the development of a balanced and harmonious plan of education on our college campus in Japan, His leadership became the central theme in the hearts of students and teachers alike. With this revelation came the unfolding of stories of courage and providence, not only from the campus, but also from alumni, workers, and friends. All of these, common conversation on the college hill, further worked in a happy cycle to provide new courage and faith for yet other obstacles.

As these accounts of God's leading became known far and near, there developed a more and more insistent demand for a collection of them to encourage Adventist workers and laymen, adult and youth, in fidelity to follow the plan of God. This volume is an attempt to meet this need and to direct the minds of men to a promise-keeping God.

Special appreciation is due President Toshio Yamagata, distinguished scholar, internationally known astrophysicist, and then dean of Japan Missionary College, who read the entire manuscript; and to Francis Millard, veteran missionary to Japan and president of the Japan Union Mission of Seventh-day Adventists, and to other workers who were helpful in checking certain stories and in developing source materials. Such assistance was particularly worthy of gratitude, since a number of the accounts came from a time of war and had been subject to unnumbered emotions and religious and nationalistic feelings, and had been retold in a variety of ways. Indeed in certain cases, to preserve accuracy and yet not offend anyone, it has been necessary to disguise names and certain minute details.

Final gratitude must be expressed to my wife, Dorothy, for her faithful and skilled editing, and to two little story hounds, Dennis and Kathleen, who were the laboratory where the stories were tested. It has been a precious and reassuring experience for us as a family to witness in this twentieth century the direction and certainty in the leading of God.

THE AUTHOR

Just to be friendly we stepped up and greeted the visitors from Japan.

When Is a Call from God?

THE story began without ceremony in the late summer of 1950. At that time I was on the faculty at Pacific Union College, where my main occupation was the education of teachers, along with some general administrative responsibilities.

One Sunday my wife and I had two guests from faraway Japan come to our house for dinner—Francis Millard, president of the Japan Union Mission, and Toshio Yamagata, dean of Japan Junior College. Elder Millard was eager to show Dean Yamagata a typical American home and also to bring greetings from Mrs. Millard, a choirmate from college days.

We had an interesting time asking questions about the Land of the Rising Sun, which then seemed as distant as the stars. Some mention had been made in a kidding manner about the possibility of my wife and I going to Japan someday, but no one took it seriously, for we were well established and cozy in our home off California's famed Silverado Trail, not far from the college campus.

After dinner and a pleasant exchange our two guests left on their busy trip. We did not expect to see them again—for a long time at least.

But apparently God had other plans. Five or six months later, in the winter of 1950, a letter came from Washington: "Japan Union Mission is in serious need of a president for their college—a man with a Doctor's degree who particularly understands teacher education. Is it possible that you might be willing to go? . . ."

I put the letter down on my desk, stunned. "How can we possibly go now?" I thought aloud.

"I beg your pardon?" my half-startled secretary inquired of her absent-minded boss.

"I was just wondering, with all there is to do here, whether this call can really be from God."

In 1939 there had been a call to Africa. My wife and I had decided to go if it was the Lord's will. But it turned out in the medical examination that Dorothy could not take quinine. And that drug was an important prophylactic for malaria in those days.

Then there were the two calls during the war, one to the Caribbean and the other to China. There were no questions about these, for the Army Medical Department had called me overseas to New Guinea and the Philippines.

We knelt more humbly than usual that night. We also decided to talk to several counselors in whom we had great confidence—the union conference president; the president of the college; members of the General Conference education staff; W. E. Nelson, of the General Conference; Dr. Mary McReynolds, the grand old mother of Pacific Union College and Loma Linda; Frederick Griggs; and Prof. Harry Washburn. Several stated that our work had just begun at Pacific Union College and that they thought we should stay there at least another several years. Only one was distinctly encouraging about accepting the call. But all advised that we go slowly, praying our way along.

I knew all too well that there was much to do at the college. Furthermore, the advice of my close friends and esteemed counselors seemed to point in one direction—to stay where I was. This looked like common sense. Nevertheless something inside seemed to say Go.

But was this the voice of the Lord? Should I ask for a sign like Gideon? One time I had talked with my good friend, George Vandeman.

"It is much better, Ray," he had cautioned, "for one to come nearer and nearer to Jesus until he is well aware of what He wants him to do."

A few days after the Washington note Dorothy and I received a letter from Japan. It was Elder Millard asking if I would be interested in going over to be president of the college. But, strangely, the letter was so worded as to indicate that he did not know anything about the call that we had received from the General Conference. We checked carefully and found this to be true. The two calls had come entirely independently! Was this an indication? We were soon to find out.

We began to make more serious inquiry in case we should go: Could a replacement be found at the end of the school year? What would we take? How long would we be gone? Should we take a car?

The last turned out to be the key question.

"You will need a car," wrote Elder Millard.

"Yes, you should have a car," others agreed, but added a caution: "Japan's customs and tax laws are changing fast. Better check."

Japan is famous for its many customs duties—fees and taxes on cars often amount to considerably more than the price of the car itself. We wrote our Japanese friends for information about this, but received no reliable answer because of the changing situation in that occupied land. "Write to the Land Transportation Bureau in Tokyo," advised the Japanese Government representative at San Francisco.

This we did, and received a courteous but indefinite reply.

"Try the Customs and Taxation Section of Japan's Ministry of Finance," the San Francisco Japanese suggested next.

The first letter to the Finance Ministry did not bring a reply. Nor did the second.

Now we *were* in a quandary.

On the one hand, it had seemed that our experience with Japanese students in schools in California, and in Hawaii, while teaching at the college extension there, could also be considered in our decision. We had learned to love the Japanese. On the other hand, we were torn by the counsel of our friends.

Meanwhile our impressions continued, increasing in strength, that we should go to Japan. But it was hard to explain this "heart feeling" to our friends. They might charge it up to "emotional thinking," and we were not inclined to make decisions "from feeling." We needed something of a more explicit nature in order to make our final decision.

Then came the experience at Yosemite. I had gone down to an education meeting at the National Park with lingering doubts about the whole Japan idea, especially after having received discouraging word about the car.

On Thursday and Friday Prof. W. H. Meier and I went to the conferences at the Ahwahnee Hotel and worked on plans to improve the teacher-education program of the college. All was pointing toward bigger things. Late Friday afternoon, before the conferences were over, we returned to our cabin in the valley to prepare for Sabbath. After bathing and evening worship we headed for supper at the famed Yosemite Lodge.

There were thoughts of the greatness of God in our minds as we walked toward the lodge.

"Who," I pondered, "could go to Yosemite Valley and not think of God?" Even the Japan problem, which had been so much in my thoughts, had momentarily given way to the inspiring panorama of the park.

For some reason, instead of heading directly toward the center door of the lodge, the one nearest the cafeteria, the professor and I walked around by way of the south entrance. As we walked up the steps to the porch three Asian men stepped out of a bus. It was easy to see from the cut of their clothing and the flat brims of their hats that they were new in America.

Just to be friendly, we stepped up, greeted them, asked them where they were from, and welcomed them to Yosemite.

"We are from Tokyo." Their sober faces could not hide their surprise and delight at having someone take an interest in them, and casual bows accented their appreciation as they followed the lodge porter, who was impatiently beckoning them down the corridor.

A few minutes later in the cafeteria we met them again and were invited to join them for supper.

A happy conversation followed, led by Mr. Nishimoto, a genteel person, a graduate of the Imperial University, and the one of the three who could speak reasonably fluent English. But none of the men revealed the reason for their visit to the States.

"Why don't you tell them about your Japan problem?" something seemed to tell me when there was a lull in the conversation. They were immediately interested. I told them completely of the car problem, the only thing that was keeping me from making a final decision.

"Is it your own car?" Mr. Nishimoto inquired.

"Yes."

"Have you had it for six months or more?"

"Yes."

"Why, that is an easy question to answer," he offered confidently. "There will not be any tax or duty on your car."

"We have heard that from several people," I spoke doubtfully. "As a matter of fact, we have heard all kinds of stories, but what we want to know are the facts."

Mr. Nishimoto turned to his colleague, Mr. Hirata, and said a few words rapidly in Japanese. He next turned to his other friend for a brief exchange.

Then, looking me straight in the eye, he said kindly but with great self-assurance, *"I can say positively that you will not have to pay any customs duty or excise tax if you take your own car to Japan."*

"How can we be absolutely sure about this?" I questioned, still the doubting Thomas.

"Because Mr. Hirata here is the man who writes the laws," Mr. Nishimoto answered.

"What did you say?"

"Mr. Hirata is the director of Customs and Taxation for the Ministry of Finance of the Japanese Government," he answered soberly.

"Mr. Shoji," he continued, "is in charge of the tax section, and my job is to direct the customs section. You can believe that what we say is all right. We will give you our cards—"

The drama of the moment was a delightful mixture of amazement, happiness, and praise to God. There seemed little for me to say after that. But the sequel made it more wonderful.

The three men were on a trip from Japan to Washington to study the customs and taxation laws of the United States Government. They had made this side trip by bus. They would be in Yosemite for only fourteen hours, from six o'clock that night to eight o'clock the next morning. "A remarkable 'coincidence,'" Professor Meier and I agreed. And before excusing ourselves we offered to show them the glories of Yosemite Valley on Sabbath morning.

The next morning, after bidding three grateful Japanese men goodbye, we headed for our appointment at Lodi Academy. Interestingly enough, the academy principal had been forced to cancel the gathering—the meeting that was the reason for our Friday evening stay at Yosemite. But God's purpose had been accomplished.

"That was a remarkable experience," Professor Meier broke the silence as we rode along the highway toward home.

"Yes, that's just about it," I was compelled to agree, with a finality and decision that through the months ahead would lead me across the sea to Japan. "It looks as if the call is from God."

There is a sequel to this story.

As if to underscore what He had already shown in bold print, God added experience to providential experience in the years that followed. Mr. Hirata has advanced until, at the writing of this book, he is Vice-Minister of Finance for Japan, the operational head of the Ministry, the most powerful nonpolitical financial figure in the nation.

Time and again he has come to the rescue of our church, helping to solve difficult tax and customs problems, lifting heavy financial burdens from the denomination in Japan. In one decision alone he determined that our national workers in Japan were exempt from income tax on their tithe. Heretofore they were subject to heavy assessments on all income.

We learned well the eternal lesson that God does not necessarily speak to us through one person or means. Rather, He often uses many avenues and multiplied circumstances to point us in the way He would have us go—all depending on our readiness and determination to find it.

"Some are worried that if their children work on the farm, their legs will become banty, just like the farmers."

Prisoners' Food

"YOU know," one of the students said to me after class one day soon after we had arrived in Japan, "we Japanese have much stronger bodies than the Americans. We have very great endurance," he gestured proudly toward the students outside on the farm.

"Is that right?" I asked.

"Yes, Japan has many records in cross-the-country races," was the answer. "I think Japanese have much more endurance.

"Then how do you account for all the tuberculosis?" I asked, knowing that Occupation medical authorities found that nine out of ten Japanese had been infected.

"I am not sure—" the youth answered hesitantly.

A few days later one of the teachers came into the office. He seemed concerned, but there was a certain smugness in his manner.

"Sensei," he began, bowing graciously, "Sensei, some of us are afraid some of the parents are not going to like to have their children working on our farm."

"Why that's too bad," I replied seriously, but probably without enthusiasm, knowing that this particular teacher was dying hard on the work aspect of the threefold plan. "What makes you think that way?"

"Well, you know many Japanese people have short legs, and sort of curved—'banty' I think you call it."

I nodded as understandingly as possible under the circumstances.

"Some are worried," he continued, "that if the students work on the farm, their legs will become banty, just like the farmers. And these days we Japanese want our children to have long, straight legs like the Americans."

This was my introduction to the problem of diet and health in Japan. For it is well known that both the dreaded tuberculosis and the bowed legs were blamed on almost anything but the chief cause—the diet.

It was hard indeed to understand how these people, subsisting on such a spare diet, could possibly be so strong and develop such great "endurance." I soon found that all this was not so. Some of the students, who were suffering from malnutrition when they first enrolled, would have to take rest periods every hour or so during their work on the farm. Although we had made sure that none of them was given heavy work, they still required the rest.

"Why is this, Sensei?" I asked Dean Yamagata one day.

"The normal Japanese diet just does not provide enough energy-giving food for a full day's work," he replied quite frankly.

I began investigating the diet immediately, and what I saw was enough to stir any nutrition-conscious individual. The students were eating three meals consisting chiefly of polished rice and a dry variety of sweet potato. The few vegetables, which were not well prepared, could usually look to their future in the garbage can.

The *status quo* was not going to be easy to change.

The Japanese had deep-seated reasons for wanting to eat their white rice, shorn as it was of nearly all its natural vitamins and minerals, and almost one sixth of its wholegrain volume.

"Why," I asked, "do intelligent people eat food like this?"

"You see," Yamagata explained, "brown rice is considered a food for prisoners and poor people, and no one wants anybody to think he is poor."

Furthermore, *genmai*, as brown rice is commonly known in Japan, was forced upon the people, along with dark bread, as a conservation measure during wartime. Ten years of being forced to eat any kind of food is likely to bring about the wrong kind of reaction.

And that was not all.

"The Japanese have a great fear of appendicitis," he continued.

It was a common belief that the coarse outer covering of *genmai* was a common cause of appendicitis, and "none of us," the students and teachers were quick to point out, "can afford to leave school for the hospital."

One of the most important factors, however, was not mentioned by anyone, and that simply was that *genmai* is much harder to chew than *hakumai* as refined rice is known. Some of the Japanese students were proud of the fact that they could down a large bowl of white rice in only two or three minutes. Obviously this could not be done with brown rice—that is, not without suffering.

It was decided that plans must be carefully made, considering all the factors, both psychological and physiological. In the first place, there must be more time given for meals. Next, some well-known authorities on nutrition must be brought in to talk first to the faculty and later to the students. Then after some questions were raised and discussion groups were "incidentally" started, the time would come for a plan to be laid before the faculty.

This was done, but it took a long time to educate against tradition. Many a time I prayed about this matter, for it seemed to me an extremely important one. It involved the economy of the college, for it was cheaper to serve brown rice to the students than white. They would eat less of the brown rice and would obtain much more benefit from it. This in turn would give the matron more money with which to diversify the diet.

All these ideas were in the plan, but it took a long time to get them across to the people. Nevertheless, once the students were thoroughly persuaded, and were convinced that it was also the plan of God, there was little protest. As usual in such cases, some of the older folks took longer than the students to accept the change. But most of them, without any pointed invitation, quickly brought their homes into line.

Help came from an unexpected source, and it became possible to begin serving whole-wheat bread instead of white.

In Kisarazu, a city of forty thousand, some seven miles from the campus, Mr. Hirose, an Adventist layman, operated a food shop that sold products of the College Bakery and Health Foods. He worked closely with the school toward educating his community in healthful eating, and was being blessed day by day.

But the Asian people are slow to change established habits. After all, *kuropan*—whole-wheat bread—was prisoners' food, and did not appeal to status-conscious Japanese.

Then Kawabe, an electrician, came into the store one day. Because of an industrial accident months before, two thirds of his stomach had been removed. After that he went from store to store trying to find food that his stomach could digest.

"Have you tried the college whole-wheat bread?" a friend suggested one day, showing him an advertisement.

"No, but maybe I will," Kawabe replied, half seriously. Almost anything was worth trying, the way he had been feeling. One week later he was a *kuropan* convert.

"It is the staff of my life," he told his customers and friends elatedly. Wherever he went, his testimony won new customers for the little health food store, and before long his experience with the *kuropan* led him to the bread of life.

The effect on the campus was electric. And the lesson was never forgotten.

As the months passed by, the program began to pay off. The students noticed that they were obtaining a greater variety, and began to make favorable comparisons with the food in their homes instead of the distasteful comparisons that some of them had made before.

"Sensei, Sensei," a student was calling outside our bedroom window at two o'clock one morning.

"Yes?" I answered half consciously.

"Sensei, can you take Imura San to Tokyo? He must be operated."

It seemed as if the old devil was hounding us, for several students did have attacks of "appendicitis," and two actually had appendectomies. Frequently we were called, usually in the middle of the night. But more often than not the writhing patient was merely having an attack of common worms—an affliction usually more painful than dangerous.

Whether appendicitis was caused by the *genmai* was a moot question, but there was no doubt that most of the Japanese thought it was. So another educational program had to be started, reminding both students and teachers that if they did not chew their food they could not be insured against appendicitis. The college has not had an appendicitis case since.

About this time the college dietitian went to a nutrition conference at which the health records of all the schools were compared. She came back with a glowing report.

"All the other schools are down here like this," said she, all smiles, and gesturing with both hands, "but ours, they said, was altogether higher than any of the others."

Naturally this made everyone happy, and once again we praised God.

A short while later a second study was made, this time by the Japan Dental Association. Once more it was determined that our college ranked by far the highest of all the schools tested.

A short time later a third study was made, this one by Dr. James Claude Thompson, of Columbia University. He came to the college and took several days to make a thorough examination of every student. He looked at the tongue, the skin, and the eyes, and then checked the results of his recent physical examination. Some weeks later, when his tabulations had been made, he reported his findings.

"The health excellence of the students at Japan Missionary College is in approximate proportion to the time they have spent there," he wrote factually.

Coming from an authoritative American specialist, this made a special impression upon the students and teachers. It paid off in many ways, with an even better attendance record. Our doors remained open even during periods when other schools about us would close completely because of influenza epidemics.

Our college, thanks to the blessing of God and our "prisoners' food," has never had to close.

Always kind, ever courteous, both Prince and Princess made an immediate and forceful impression on the students and teachers.

The Coming of the Prince

ONE evening at a conference of the International Student Association in downtown Tokyo I was introduced to His Imperial Highness Prince Takamatsu, brother of the Emperor. What made the Prince's presence especially important was the fact that the Emperor himself is not allowed by his counselors to go to such occasions. The Prince was the social ambassador of the Imperial Throne.

In the course of the evening we were seated at a small table with the Prince, his lovely Princess, and some prominent educators. The Prince joined readily in casual conversation, and before long was inquiring about the nature of our school.

"Would you like to visit us?" I asked, taking courage.

"I would be delighted," he replied.

"When would it be convenient?" I asked boldly, but inwardly doubtful.

"You set the date," was the ready response.

"I would be grateful for your address," I suggested, handing him my pen and little black appointment book.

"Just give me a month's notice," he noted as he marked his brief address in Japanese *Kanji*.

I seemed to be holding my breath almost all the way home that night—could hardly wait to tell the school family of the possibility.

The American teachers were all pleased at the prospect, not so much by the fact that the Prince would come to visit us, important as that is in Japan, but that something important might actually be accomplished by his visit. We had been having a difficult time raising the campus standards of beauty, neatness, and order, which had fallen so low in the difficult war years. We urgently needed motivation for the present, and precedent for the future. This might well supply both, we thought.

Even though Shintoism, which involves the worship of the imperial family, was on the decline, and although Buddhism and the other isms of Japan had little influence upon our students, there was still a deep reverence for the Emperor and anyone closely connected with him. The old days were gone forever, but the people of Japan would still go to the shrines of their emperors much as an American goes to the Lincoln Memorial or the Britisher to Westminster.

But if I thought that I was going to get any unusual reaction out of the Japanese teachers, I was in for disappointment. When I mentioned the possibility they smiled and nodded, but apparently thought that this was just another hopeful idea of their new president. I began to realize that the less said the better until an actual appointment was made. For if the Prince did not come, what then?

A few months later a building program was in progress. It would be completed about the first of May. This coincided with the approximate time of the year when the roots of the college had been set in 1897—fifty-five years before. Therefore it was decided that we would have a Founders' Day program and would invite the Prince.

I called the secretariat at the Prince's palace.

"The Prince said he would be open to an invitation," I reminded them, referring to the commitment the Prince had made several months before. With cultured Japanese such a promise is usually kept, especially with schools, for in Japan teachers are held in great respect. They are called *Sensei,* literally, "born before," because they are to be assiduously followed, thoughtfully emulated.

"I will consider it a pleasure to visit you," the Prince answered through his courtiers. "I will be happy to talk over plans for the occasion at your convenience."

The date for the big event was readily fixed at May 6. Furthermore, the Prince was willing to give a talk, something he did not usually do. The big appointment was on!

A few days later a secretary called. "May His Highness have a copy of your book *Education?*"

"It will be there tomorrow," I promised.

The book had been mentioned in previous conversation, and the Prince wanted to read it as a basis for his remarks at our Founders' Day ceremony. From what he said later it was apparent that he had read well.

The May 6 program was mentioned to the students and teachers with routine chapel announcements.

"His Imperial Highness Prince Takamatsu"—there was a deathly silence—"will visit our college the day of May 6, from eleven in the morning." The oh's and the gasps even surprised themselves, for usually the Japanese are undemonstrative in public gatherings.

The activity on the campus was something to behold. Trees were pruned. New waste containers were made to be placed at strategic places. Unsightly collections of rubbish, lumber, et cetera, were disposed of. Shacks and outbuildings were either demolished or repaired. Grass was cut far beyond the normal expanse of the lawn. Floors were scrubbed with sodium hydroxide and waxed several times. The students and teachers made it a college rule to walk on classroom floors only with slippers. Special character-education programs were developed for both chapel and worships. A startling change came over the entire group.

By the time the Prince arrived, six weeks later, the campus was in all its beauty a dream picture come true. Students and teachers had learned many spiritual lessons. The students began to realize that the school was more important than they thought. If it was important enough to be recognized by their Imperial Prince it must be quite "something," for he seldom went so far to such places.

It also offered an opportunity to compare their reverence for the Emperor with their reverence for God, who also wanted things clean. Their sense of pride of ownership went up as clearly as a rocket on a moonless July 4 night.

As a public relations gesture the visit also was to pay off considerably more than had been anticipated. Its effect was to benefit the college for years. As soon as the announcement was made and invitations to dignitaries extended, a unanimous and happy reaction from educational officials, businessmen, and community leaders was observed.

Some were more excited than we. A number visited the campus ahead of time. Local police and detectives from the nearby communities and the prefectural office came out along with others from the Japanese Government and the palace to make sure that all preparations were right for the Prince. Nothing was spared.

But there was one great problem. Several teachers came to me after faculty worship one morning.

"Whatever are we going to wear for this occasion?" they pleaded almost in unison. "What will we do? Shall we rent afternoon clothes?"

In Japan such occasions are usually marked with great formality, and those who cannot afford to buy formal clothes—striped trousers, swallow-tailed coats, and similar clothing—for such occasions must go to clothing rental stores and become outfitted. This was expensive in postwar Japan, where such clothes were not plentiful.

One of two things had to be done: Everybody had to adjust to the Prince or the Prince would have to adjust to us. It was decided that from our point of view, and the standpoint of our collective pocketbook, the latter would be by far the best procedure, depending of course on the Prince.

The matter was frankly presented to the Prince.

"I would much prefer informal wear," he smiled. "I will wear a dark business suit."

The standard was set. Everyone was relieved, greatly relieved. What clothes they did have were pressed and clean on that great day.

We could hardly see how we could adequately use the Prince's time for the entire day at the college, so arranged for him to make an inspection tour of the nearby United Nations air base, where the commander had arranged a parade and some demonstrations with jet and propellerdriven planes. This gave our day a good start, for the Prince is an aviation enthusiast.

Back at the college, as the hour approached for the Prince's arrival, everyone was tense and alert. It was a lesson to us as we thought of the coming of the Prince of Peace and the urgency that we should have in preparing for His coming.

The Prince had made his way out to the college from his palace, nearly fifty miles away. On that entire route the police of each city and village were alerted and posted along the highway at frequent intervals. At the college we were constantly informed by a radio police car of the Prince's progress. We knew just when he was leaving Tokyo, the moment he passed through Ichikawa, and then Chiba City, Goi, Anegasaki, and finally the time he was to arrive, by way of the air base, at the college campus.

All were especially happy and surprised when the Prince's sedan drove onto the campus to find that he had brought with him his lovely Princess, herself from the dynasty of Japan's great Tokugawa Shogunate. Always kind, ever courteous to even the poorest of the neighborhood urchins, both Prince and Princess made an immediate and forceful impression on the students and teachers.

An American vegetarian meal had been prepared for the dignitaries, who included the prefectural governor, educational leaders, business and professional men and women. It was pleasant to note how friendly and how much at home they seemed. The Prince came back to the buffet for a second helping of vegetarian cutlets.

"These are some of the best breaded veal cutlets I have eaten," he enthused in his usual excellent English.

"Those," I replied, "are made from Japanese wheat!"

It was entertaining to all to watch royalty astonished.

"How do you do this?" he asked, eyes wide open.

"We will show you at our College Food Industry after the program," I promised.

Promptly at two o'clock all took their places on the dais before the crowd assembled on the lawn of our new administration building. Blessed by God, it was a thoroughly enjoyable occasion from beginning to end. The remarks of the Prince were noteworthy.

"It is a heartfelt joy," he began, "to meet with Dr. Moore, the teachers, and students of this school, which is said to be a school for souls. It is so because I understand that this school is based upon the profound and excellent principles of education as taught by Ellen G. White, who developed a system of education for the harmonious development of the head, the heart, and the hand.

"It is in a school like this that we can properly say that a new life is brought into being. We hear that nature is the mirror of love, but man's spirit needs a constant training. And it really is a remarkable thing that here is presented before us such a beautiful and unadulterated harmony of nature and man. True education is to learn of eternal wisdom.

"I have heard that in the history of Christianity, salvation through faith and love has led the world through the problem of sin. Now, when the fate of the modern society is bringing fear, uncertainty, and suffering, we are trying to overcome them and find the way by seeking salvation through faith, as Saint Augustine besought the establishment of the kingdom of God when the ancient world was about to collapse.

"So we must step forward by overcoming, when today we in the twentieth century are about to decide for eternal life or death, either light or darkness; and it is none other than education through love, I believe, that, as an answer to our quest, will produce the joy for which we are looking. I believe that your school may be the place where this most important proposition is to be studied and solved.

"I pray that you will earnestly strive on toward this end."

His thoughts were echoed by several distinguished educators that day, including Japan's Minister of Education. But especially noteworthy were the remarks of Professor Nagatoro, college president, chairman of the board of education of Chiba prefecture, and head of all the private schools, easily the most important educator in the state:

"... I would like to encourage you earnestly *to become the leaders of the new Japan with your great message, with your worldwide view, and with your love and your religious conviction.*"

God be praised for the great insight He has given to these men! The students were deeply impressed, and the teachers too. They realized that they were part of an important program. A testimony meeting a short time later was revealing.

From that day on, the campus of Japan Missionary College has been one of the show places of the prefecture. But more important, the true significance of our program began to dawn in the hearts of our students and teachers. The Prince had done more than he ever knew to establish a program of true education in the Land of the Rising Sun.

Dr. Mizuno had been used by God to bring Japan Union Mission through one of its most serious dilemmas.

The Providential Dr. Waterfield

THERE was excitement on the campus, especially among the teachers. Today a distinguished guest was coming out to visit us. He was important to us for many reasons.

On the dot at eleven o'clock the train pulled up to the Naraha station and off stepped Dr. Tsunekichi Mizuno with one of his younger professors from Tamagawa University. Tamagawa had come to be an important word on our campus in recent months. And Dr. Mizuno was the principal reason. God had done much for us through this great Japanese educator.

After a brief tour of the campus, our guests, along with Dean Yamagata and our teacher-training man, Professor Funada, sat down with my wife and me for dinner. Everything was spread beautifully, and the big Lazy Susan was carefully set in the middle of our round table, adorned with a *gochiso*—Japanese for an especially delicious meal.

Dr. Mizuno could speak English well and took special pleasure in talking in our language. This made the occasion especially pleasant, for there was not the usual tenseness that comes when some of the conversation must be translated.

The younger professor was especially fascinated with the Lazy Susan, an unusually large one that held the several dishes of our main course. Playfully he turned the circular tray, not realizing that it was set in the roller bearings of an airplane wheel. It responded more quickly than was anticipated, and whirled around.

Then, oops, it happened. A spoon sticking out from one of the dishes hit Dr. Mizuno's glass, full of water. Over it went—right into his lap.

Mrs. Moore was embarrassed and ran for a towel. But the old professor just roared.

"You know what my name means, don't you?" he spoke out through his laugh.

Several guesses followed, a pretense in confusion.

"My name means 'waterfield.'"

Then we all laughed. "What a happy way to put his hostess at ease," I thought as we resumed our meal.

And a thoughtful man he was. He had been God's instrument to bring the college, and indeed our entire educational program in Japan, through some of its most serious dilemmas. At one time he had taken the entire issue of one of Japan's important educational journals to write up our school and its plan. Now God used him once more when in our extremity the accreditation of the college and our whole educational program for Japan and Okinawa were at stake.

A serious problem had only recently arisen. The Japan Union Mission must have church school teachers, and those teachers, by government order, must be credentialed by the Ministry of Education. In order for them to be so credentialed they must take their teacher-education work in a college or university that was accredited by the government. After the Occupation the Education Ministry began once more to put pressure on parochial schools.

This was the one great problem that we had long dreaded—accreditation. The college had been accredited only as a "miscellaneous" junior college and also as a high school. But to have to meet all the stringent government requirements seemed an impossibility.

After talking the matter over with Dean Yamagata and Professor Funada I realized that accreditation with the Japanese Government was entirely out of the question unless we sacrificed the principles of the college and the threefold program that we were so earnestly trying to work out.

There was only one thing to do. That was the same thing that had been done so many times before. "God, show us the way," we prayed together. The whole problem was laid out very frankly before Him. He was reminded of His promises.

It had been during the harrowing days just before World War II that the college was in deep trouble. It could not meet the complex demands of the Ministry of Education then either—that is, if it wanted to comply with the requirements of God.

At that time it was a matter of freedom, and freedom was long gone with the process of "thought control" that had been established by the Ministry of Education. It had been a dark hour indeed for our college and for Christian education in Japan. All that had been gained during the more than forty years since the beginning of school seemed to be on hell's auction block. Again, later, Dr. Mizuno interfered in behalf of the college.

He did not say at that time how he had found the book he had read. That was to come out in our living room a number of years later. Nevertheless, Dr. Mizuno, director of social education for Japan, and later director of Japan's National Museum of Science, knew the plan of God.

Now after the war, when the tramp, tramp of boots had been replaced by the sound of rubber-sandaled feet in the college halls, we were once more in trouble. It was obvious that we must have teachers, and they must not be trained in outside schools, for what kind of education would they give our church schools? We were at our extremity, so this was God's opportunity. We could not forget how He had led in the past.

Now, nearly fifteen years after the previous experience, we tried to establish a sound relationship with the Ministry of Education. Unfortunately Dr. Mizuno was no longer there. It seemed that all our approaches led only to blind alleys.

"You had better change your program to fit the government's," some admonished.

"You will find that Japan is no place to innovate," others warned.

Others, including some of our own leaders, suggested that we take on non-Adventist teachers. Still others put forth the idea that we place ourselves under other highly accredited universities. But none of these plans could possibly be the will of God. How could we expect His blessings if we presumed against His will?

Faced with no alternatives, we prayed more earnestly than ever.

Then in our extremity God stepped in.

On Founders' Day, 1952, the guests of Japan Missionary College were the Imperial Prince and Princess Takamatsu. Being the brother and personal representative of the Emperor, his presence meant much wherever he visited. Many important businessmen, government officials, and educators gathered at the college to bask in the presence of the Prince and Princess. One of these was a Ministry of Education official who had already been of help to us. He was Dr. Jintaro Kataoka, liaison officer with the United Nations.

Yamagata was talking with him about our accreditation problem.

"Why don't you affiliate with Chiba University?" he suggested.

"We thought of that, but it will not work out with our educational plan," Yamagata answered frankly.

"I used to teach at a university that might help you— Tamagawa," he offered next.

"We know Tamagawa's fine reputation," Yamagata conceded, "but I doubt whether they would come to our rigid terms."

"But," insisted Dr. Kataoka kindly, "Tamagawa's ideals are really much like yours. You must go and contact either the dean of teacher education or the director of extensions there."

With many reservations in their minds, Yamagata and Funada went to Tamagawa University. After the traditional Japanese greetings they were ushered into the office of the director of extensions, who, it turned out, was also the teacher-education head. To their great surprise and joy they were introduced to Dr. Mizuno, the faithful friend of Adventist education. The men uttered a silent prayer of thanksgiving to God. And thus was renewed a friendship that was destined to lead to one of the most remarkable and providential experiences we had ever seen or heard.

With his ready knowledge of the plan of Japan Missionary College, Dr. Mizuno was almost immediately ready to work out a satisfactory relationship between the schools. But there were many things that stood in the way.

"We are in the strange position," Yamagata apologized, "of asking a favor, but having to insist on its conditions."

"What are those conditions?" The old professor was solicitous.

"In the first place," Yamagata began, "all courses must be consistent with our principles. Second, the basic teaching must be done by our own teachers."

Dr. Mizuno nodded.

"Third, we cannot afford the high costs that usually go with such benefits. And, finally, we believe you understand why we cannot enter into any affiliations that would involve meetings or other professional obligations on our Sabbath."

"I do not see any serious obstacles here," the older man mused as he set about to suggest a plan.

The impasse, however, turned out to be Dr. Mizuno's fellow professors. They were not acquainted with our philosophy of education, and were unsympathetic with any little college on the peninsula across Tokyo Bay. When Dean Yamagata's terms were outlined, they were sure they wanted nothing further to do with Japan Missionary College.

But Dr. Mizuno is a man of great conviction.

"I know this school well," he pointed out. "We have nothing to lose in giving them a chance. And maybe we have something to gain."

The men were adamant.

"Just put them on their own merits. I'll take the responsibility," he insisted.

The men reluctantly agreed. And the dates for the entrance examinations of the first ten Japan Missionary College student teachers were set.

There was much prayer in the Japan Missionary College camp those days. Much was at stake for our work over all Japan. Yet we knew that Tamagawa had earned a stern reputation for its entrance examinations. Even with a selected list of applicants, at least one third were routinely failed. And here were our ten students, whose chief study had been the Word of God, taking an examination which assumed that they knew the philosophies of men.

They spent an entire day writing the tests. And then waited with foreboding until the day the mail boy would bring the news in fat brown envelopes.

All ten failed!

There was much sorrow in the camp of Israel when that news arrived. We talked some more with God. Just what did He have in mind in leading us through all of this embarrassment? At least we thought He was leading.

Professor Funada went sixty miles to Tamagawa to see.

"We told you so!" fellow professors reminded Dr. Mizuno.

They saw no possibility of working out a relationship with that little school. How could they have better evidence for their conclusions? And after all, there was Tamagawa's reputation to uphold. They did have something to lose now.

But Dr. Mizuno thought differently.

"You must realize," he said, addressing his professors, "that the method of education at Japan Missionary College is entirely different. Their background, their tests, their teaching—all is different. You must let these ten students take our teacher-education course."

This was challenged by the professors, who thought him a little out of his usual good judgment.

"I told you I will take the responsibility personally," Dr. Mizuno urged.

Arrangements were finally concluded for the teaching of certain key Tamagawa education courses at Japan Missionary College. Each of these courses represented the Best in modern educational methods. Japan Missionary College teachers taught them in their own classrooms.

But both teachers and students felt the great pressure of trying to uphold both the name of their beloved college and the personal reputation of Dr. Mizuno. In fact, some of them became so worried about it that they momentarily forgot about the God who was arranging all this. And they came with a request.

"We are required to work twenty hours a week," they said.

This was so, for all scholarship students at Japan Missionary College must work at least that much. And all these were scholarship students—other students were required to work only eighteen hours.

"Well," they continued, "we don't see how we can keep up our work time and yet have time to study. There is a lot depending on us."

There was hesitation, and the feeling of tenseness tightened.

'We would like to be excused from part of our work program."

This was a sobering thought to the men of the administration.

"Let's pray about it," one suggested.

The students readily agreed. Rising, after a brief and thoughtful prayer, they waited expectantly for their answer.

"Whom does the success of this test depend upon more, you or *God?*"

"God, of course," came the answer.

"Whose plan are we following here, ours or God's?"

"God's."

"Did you ever hear of Daniel, or Joseph, or Esther, or——?"

The thoughtful students needed no more questions. They realized quickly that their situation compared well to that of Daniel and his three companions when they had asked Melzar to help them in their accreditation with King Nebuchadnezzar. What if those Hebrew worthies had for a moment let God down? This was just such a critical time for Adventists in Japan.

As these thoughts went through the minds of the students and teachers, they began to realize how much they could lose by departing from God's plan one iota. They were reminded again of a gem they had heard before: "Success in education depends on fidelity in carrying out the Creator's plan," and that God would give them "wisdom from above."

Bowing in the traditional gesture of courtesy, they excused themselves and went to work.

And they worked harder than before. They studied too. Worries were put away. Whichever way things went now, they at least knew that it would be their Creator's will.

And soon His will was shown—gloriously.

At the end of the first term the quarterly Tamagawa examinations were taken. There was some quickening of the pulse as we awaited those scores of corrected tests. We knew that the average grade at the university was strictly C. One professor had the reputation of permitting only one B in each class! And classes by extension were notoriously graded down.

Finally the report from the university arrived: The ten students from Japan Missionary College stood at the top of Tamagawa's teacher-education scholarship list. All of the grades were A's and B's.

Dr. Mizuno smiled at his professors. They were astonished. Ten failures had become ten top students by the standard of one of Japan's elite universities. They bowed to Dr. Mizuno. "Japan Missionary College is *very* good," they conceded, asking for leave to visit the little college "to see how it is done."

Japan Missionary College's reputation was established in Tamagawa. God's reputation was established at Japan Missionary College. The accreditation question had been answered.

They went down one hundred and ninety-eight feet, and still no water!

Providence on the Campus

JAPAN MISSIONARY COLLEGE needed water. The little well was not supplying enough.

"If you insist that your students and teachers work together three hours every day, your enrollment will fall," had been the warning. But the closer God's plan was followed, the more He prospered the school. More students came to school, and soon there were nearly twice as many as there had been before, with even larger numbers in immediate prospect.

Because it was desired to make the students healthy, they had been asked to drink at least six glasses of water every day. A campaign for cleanliness both in body and in mind was conducted—one of the specifications of the Creator's plan. But all this required water. And there was not enough.

The faculty guarded and saved money, yen by yen (yen is the money used in Japan). Finally there was enough to drill a well and to buy a pump. Everyone was excited, for this was already God's well. His blessings had made it a necessity. His rewards were bringing possibility.

The well men came. And they began to drill. Down they went, ten, twenty, thirty feet.

"We should strike good water at sixty feet," the driller prophesied. Down, down some more—fifty, sixty, seventy-five—but no water. A hundred feet, still no water. Everyone began to be afraid.

But, like Poe's persistent ravens, the men kept on drilling.

They went on to a hundred and fifty feet, a hundred and sixty, a hundred and seventy, a hundred and eighty. Now we were really worried, for we had only enough money to go two hundred feet. And that would take the very last yen we had. Down they went, slowly, slowly, as the Japanese heavy hand drills must go. A hundred ninety-eight, a hundred ninety-nine, and still no water.

Students and faculty alike had a little talk with God. We reminded Him what He had promised us—that if we followed His will, He would bless us.

Inch by inch they drilled. And then, just short of two hundred feet—almost at the end of our money, too—water gushed up, a great stream of it, up through the well to within sixty feet of the top. God had given us a fine underground stream.

But now a new perplexity was mixed with our praises. Up with the water came some fine bluish sand. In our glasses, in our kettles, in our tubs—it settled wherever we poured the water. And, worst of all, the water had a sickening taste, just like rotten eggs.

"Apparently we have struck a sulphur formation," the analyst reported. "The sand will be gone in about six weeks," he assured us.

Sure enough, in six weeks it was all gone.

"But what about the taste of the water?" the analyst was asked.

"Ah, that is quite another matter," he remonstrated. "I made no promises about the taste of the water. That is your It was an awkward situation. The students were being asked to drink a lot of water for health and for God, yet how could they drink this revolting liquid?

What to do? There was no more money. Back we went to the God who had laid out our plan for us in the first place. We reminded Him of His instructions to us, of His promise for our success. We reminded Him of the need for water. We reminded Him that our money was gone. We reminded Him too that we realized that He owned everything, and that He could do anything.

The next morning early we went out to the faucets to drink our "morning portion" of water. Our stomachs were tense as usual and our minds subconsciously set for that rotten-egg water.

But something was different. Very different indeed. The water had no taste at all.

Hurriedly, some water was sent to be tested by some laboratories in Tokyo, and the test reports came back that the water was pure—so pure in fact that we don't have to boil the water at all at Japan Missionary College like they have to do so many places in Japan.

Our wonderful God had again kept His promise. As He had done for Moses in the wilderness, so He had done for us.

Today the teachers and students of Japan Missionary College and all the visitors that come to the campus drink freely from the Miracle Well.

"I understand, but you see we Japanese must maintain very high standards."

Winning the Mombusho

IT LOOKED as if the education program was in for a really rugged experience. The future of the work depended greatly on our school. It was possible, after God's providence with Dr. Mizuno, to provide teachers, but special government permits had to be obtained before a school could operate. This time our big *jama*—obstacle—was the Mombusho.

The Japanese educators loved bigness. All over the country they had consolidated schools. But especially in the cities, where people were crowded like raisins in a cardboard box, they had counted on large schools to meet the needs of their students.

These city-bound educators could not understand how a small school could operate—especially one with more than one grade to a teacher. On the other hand, Adventist educators did not see how they could possibly develop large schools. In our churches there would sometimes be six, eight, ten, or twelve students only. A school of six classrooms and six teachers could hardly be set up for this number of students. Indeed it was difficult enough for so small a school to pay the salary of one teacher, to take care of the expenses of the school, and to provide a single classroom.

"We are anxious to help Japan," we volunteered to a high Mombusho official.

"I understand, but you see we Japanese must maintain very high standards," he replied loftily. The inference was clear.

"We are happy to meet your standards," we reassured him. "This is merely a question of method. We are quite willing to have our students measured against others."

"But you see the trend in Japan is away from small schools—just like America," he continued. "I am afraid your case is hopeless."

With a tone of finality he moved to his telephone and went on with another item of business without even the usual Asian deference to guests. He had made it clear all right— as clear as a tropical pool—that we didn't stand a chance. He was determined that there must be one classroom for each grade regardless of the number of pupils. We knew that we didn't stand a chance unless we gained the favor of this powerful Mombusho, the head school office of the nation— Japan's Ministry of Education.

We were driven to our knees, not once but many times, over this matter. We searched the Scriptures, and again and again were brought back to the first verses in Deuteronomy 28, and especially the thirteenth verse. We were promised that if we followed the instructions of God, He would make us the head and not the tail.

We also remembered the statement on page 50 of the book *Education,* "With us, as with Israel of old, success in education depends on fidelity in carrying out the Creator's plan. Adherence to the principles of God's word will bring as great blessings to us as it would have brought to the Hebrew people."

We determined to learn where, if at all, we were coming short of His plans. We wanted to make it right in order that we would be completely qualified for His blessings. So we prayed and planned without ceasing.

Miss Ethel Young, of the Far Eastern Division education office, had come to the college a few months before and worked intensively with our Japanese educators in developing a *Teachers' Guide.* This book was planned to help our church school teachers understand how to teach several grades in one classroom.

"The teachers won't use it," was the warning. "They want only one grade to a room. Just wait and see!"

"Nothing ventured, nothing gained," was our reaction.

These teachers, strongly set against such a classroom, were unaware of the fact that 35 per cent of Japan's public schoolrooms were multigrade.

After much intensive work the *Guide* was prepared, translated, and printed. Almost immediately it made a sharp impression upon some of the prefectural educational offices. But Mombusho was as immovable as Fujiyama, Japan's great god mountain. No matter how diligently we hammered away, the granite we did chisel off always seemed soon to be covered with snow.

After World War II the Japanese schools were controlled by the Americans. Now that the Occupation was over, Japan's educators were determined to assert themselves. American suggestions were generally sidetracked now, and would-be helpers were shown the "No help needed" sign.

This prejudice is easy to understand. Under the Occupation both American and Japanese education offices had generated so many rules and requirements that it seemed like two big families out for a picnic with a one-family car. One rule was sitting on the lap of another and the situation was so tight that no one could move.

But we were faced with the necessity of crowding the picnic car even more. The government course was difficult enough—more than twice as much required material as we demanded of students in America—to which Adventists must add Bible subjects.

This dilemma was compounded with the realization that our schools must begin small, and that only one teacher could usually be provided for each church school. The government insisted that this could not be done, and by their methods they were right. But God gave us courage. The city educators at Mombusho had somehow not remembered the more than one out of three of their own government schools. How were they operating?

I had tramped like a traveling salesman from official to official in the prefectures where we wanted to start our schools. Carefully our wares were described—the type of church schools that had been so successful in America and elsewhere. But the Occupation armies were now gone, and the Japanese were less interested in American ideas than they had been during the first years after World War II.

But God wanted our schools to be developed. That was a certainty. And He wanted them kept as much like family schools as possible. It was sure that He meant exactly what He said when He promised that success depends upon fidelity in carrying out His plans.

My real concern had been the attitude of our own teachers. They still wanted to teach only in the traditional Japanese way—one teacher for each classroom. Nevertheless, little by little the Spirit of God worked on their hearts, and our schools began to blossom as the "impossible" became workable in their minds.

"But what shall we do about developing *new* schools?" the ministers worried.

God's answer was the *Teachers' Guide.* Some of the prefectural educational officials had become intensely interested in this well-prepared book, which had been presented to them in making application for the establishment of our schools. Some, anxious to see its plan in action, gladly accepted an invitation to visit the several church schools already established. They noted well the lively results, the sweet spirit, and the absence of moral problems.

Soon more and more prominent educators and businessmen began to speak out in favor of our schools. The answer, the sure answer to our prayers, began to be evident.

In the spring of 1954 things really began to happen. Some of the educators who had come to Japan Missionary College invited the teachers to present our school plan before their state teachers' institutes.

The teachers prayed and planned carefully.

Present at these institutes were representatives of the Ministry of Education of the Japanese Government. God's indirect method was much better than our direct approach— the officials of the antagonistic Mombusho were traveling hundreds of miles to observe our plan in action. This was exactly what we had wanted.

"May we visit your school?" they asked Mrs. Funada, after watching her institute demonstrations.

"Certainly, we would be delighted."

"When is best for you?"

"Anytime."

Her answer seemed to surprise them, for most educators made unusual preparations for such visiting dignitaries.

A short while later two representatives of the Ministry of Education visited the school. This could have meant almost anything three months before, particularly with the criticism the school had been receiving. But this time the visitors were seeking to find out how to better organize and teach in their small schools, and they were the Mombusho officers in charge of the small schools of the nation!

The staff, led by Mrs. Funada, sat down with them, carefully explained our program and demonstrated in the campus classroom where six grades are taught in one room. Angels must have been at her side. Expressions of doubt changed to enthusiasm, and the teachers were immediately invited to the Ministry of Education for further meetings. They were to advise on the national revision program for Japan's small public schools. The atmosphere was beginning to warm in the higher reaches.

But this was only the beginning. Mrs. Funada and our teachers were then invited to national government institutes—not only those sponsored by the states but by the Mombusho itself.

One day while at our institute in Fukui the government educators approached Mrs. Funada.

"Would you mind if we use yours as a model school?"

"I beg your pardon?" she asked incredulously, remembering our days of hardship under these men.

"We would like to designate yours a model multigrade school."

"Why surely," she agreed, trying hard to conceal at least some of the exuberance in her heart.

And so it became a model for small schools of the nation, for inspection by teachers from all over Japan. In the providence of God our rubber hammer had broken down the granite mountain.

"We are not that good," we agreed among ourselves as we pondered the great opportunity, "but God's plan is."

With scant equipment, simple buildings, and little or no heat throughout the cold. Japan winters, our teachers operated happily, without complaint, for they were men and women of God. They were selected as carefully as ministers are selected, and educated as completely as possible in the plan of the Master Teacher.

It was the complete dedication of these teachers, their willingness to discard centuries-old traditions of Japan, and their complete adherence to the high standards of God that brought us the fulfillment of His promise in Deuteronomy 28:13: "The Lord shall make thee the head, and not the tail." God had led the way in winning the Mombusho.

"Let's slap Ueda and see what he does!"

The Chosen Three

THE near-sacred doors of Toho Gakuin were open again. This preparatory school, one of the most exclusive in the nation, catered primarily to sons of army and navy officers. The military had controlled the nation, and nothing was too good for their children, especially their sons.

But recently some changes had been made. And drastic ones they were, for World War II had just been closed on the deck of the U.S. battleship *Missouri*.

Only the healthiest and most astute of army and navy children were permitted now to enter the door of Toho. Sons of diplomats, businessmen, professional people, and just about anyone else could compete for the near-sacred privilege of walking its halls and sitting at the feet of its carefully selected sensei.

Despite the privilege and security that the students of Toho merited, these were days of doubt and embarrassment for the bright young men. Doubt, for with the Occupation army taking over, they hardly knew what was going to happen to their country next. Embarrassment, because they, the heirs of the Rising Sun, were now subject to the dictum of the educators of a foreign country. That was enough to embarrass even the youngest son of an officer of the imperial forces.

But youth of the stalwart quality of these young men were not the kind to wander aimlessly or to sit and wait. Inventive always, a number of them set about to ingratiate themselves in a forthright way with the conquerors. This surely must be the best thing to do, they thought, especially after their god-emperor had come down from his throne to humble himself at the doorstep of the conquering general. And what better way was there to establish themselves with the Army of Occupation than to learn its language? This they set about to do.

It was during these strange happenings that Ueda San, the son of a prominent army colonel, heard one day of an American sensei out at the Adventist mission compound who was conducting some youth meetings in English and teaching English for Japanese students. Posthaste he headed for the class, and almost immediately he developed a liking for

Mr. Adams, the tall American man, who, he was surprised to find, treated him in a fatherly way. There was not a breath of condescension at all.

The experience that Ueda San was enjoying with nine others at the "Bible study English school" was too good to keep to himself. He determined that if possible he would take with him to the next class his two pals: Ando San, the son of another army colonel, and Nakajima San, whose father was a major general.

The boys drank in the English instruction. They appreciated this unusual opportunity to learn the American language from an American himself, and with no charge at all! But when it came to the youth meetings, the two newcomers were not quite so friendly.

They attended faithfully all right, for they felt that they were obligated to keep face with Mr. Adams if they wanted to learn English. But they would chide Ueda San every time he seriously attempted to discuss the things they had heard at the young people's meeting.

"Amen," they would say in derision when he seemed to be impressed with a special truth at Mr. Adams' Bible study, "Amen, Amen." Time and again they would repeat it when Ueda San expressed an opinion of almost any kind until the situation became almost unbearable to the youth.

After all, no young person enjoys such jibes, but especially a Japanese youth whose self-respect—"face" he calls it—is just about the most sacred thing he possesses. Indeed, he will often do strange things, and extreme, in order to protect it, even to the point of suicide or murder.

Sometimes in the middle of the week when teachers called the roll at the beginning of class and someone was reported absent because of sickness, one of the boys would jab Ueda San.

"It must be Sabbath," they would say. "Amen, Amen."

But the youth was undeterred. After all, the Man whom he was now following had been hurt a lot worse. The Spirit of God was gripping his heart with something more important than the American language.

During one youth meeting the two mischief-makers learned from the American teacher that "a Christian loves his enemies," and if slapped on one side of his face, he would even turn his other cheek rather than cause trouble. Mr. Adams had told how any sincere Christian should do the same.

"Let's have some fun," Nakajima suggested to Ando on their way home.

"For example?"

"Let's slap Ueda and see what he does!"

The Chosen Three

Sure enough one day while joking with him, Nakajima slapped him. Startled, Ueda nevertheless smiled at them and shrugged off the experience with as little embarrassment as he could.

On another occasion they heard how some infamous men had spit upon the face of Christ, an act absolutely intolerable to the Japanese. Yet Christ had not remonstrated. Jestingly, some friends tried this also on the fervent young convert. The results were surprisingly the same!

About this time Ueda San had trouble at home.

"You stay away from those Christian dogs," his father warned.

"You are asking something I cannot do," was the pious answer.

"I will teach you what you cannot do," his father retorted angrily.

Ueda San was forced for a while to leave home.

All these events began to make an impress upon the hearts of his fellow students, but especially upon Ando San and Nakajima San. The next Friday night they were unusually attentive. Only this time they were seeking for spiritual meat, instead of a bone of contention. Their parents noted the difference, and even became suspicious. But these were days when the military had lost its face and some fathers were more cautious than bold.

One day, at the invitation of the American teacher, Ueda San determined to enroll for Christian education at Japan Missionary College. Ando San and Nakajima San went with him.

All met opposition, but all were men of character. They had been weighed and chosen by the hand of God. And each with his own talents and in his own way graduated from that Christian college to become leaders for God in new Japan, well in advance of their years—sons of the Emperor of the Universe.

"You can't graduate without this examination, and I am not changing it for you or anyone else."

Yasushi and God

THERE was a knock on the office door. In a moment Yasushi Tamura stood before my desk, a slightly built Japanese youth, bowing in the modern manner. "I have a problem, Dr. Moore."

"Sit down, Tamura San." I offered him a chair, wondering for a quick moment why this Adventist boy was coming to me. For he was not one of our students. He was a medical student at a great state university.

"My final examination on the eye comes next Sabbath," he began, the smile of fellowship on his finely chiseled face turning to an expression of concern. It was indeed something to be concerned about.

"But," he hastened to add, "I am not going to take it then. I am going to keep the Sabbath. *I am going to keep the Sabbath!*"

Yasushi had been an Adventist for about five years. For four of those years he had been a medical student at Chiba University, one of the top medical schools in Japan, and well-known throughout world medical circles. This college accepts only one out of every twenty selected applicants.

Six years before, while a student at the exclusive Tokyo High School, Yasushi had been sweating out a mixture of studies that had been developed by the American Occupation along with the Japan Ministry of Education. Tokyo High School had the reputation of being the strictest high school in the nation. And in Japan it is a privilege to go to high school, for compulsory education includes only the ninth grade. One day his younger brother, Hiromu, came running into the house.

"I have really been learning some wonderful things down at the mission!" he exclaimed.

"Please be quiet, Hiromu," Yasushi complained. "Can't you see I am studying?"

"But, really, this is important," was the younger brother's answer.

"There is nothing quite so important right now as my math," Yasushi retorted.

Then, stepping up to his brother in a confidential way, Hiromu asked, "What would you think if I told you that before long this whole world is going to be changed by the God who made it?"

"I would think you were crazy."

"Well, you are scientific-minded, aren't you?" the younger brother challenged.

There was no response.

"Well, if you want to turn your mind away from truth, you can go right on being dumb."

But Yasushi never once turned down a challenge. "Where did you get all of this stuff?" he asked, finally showing the interest that had begun to blossom secretly a few moments before. He became so interested in Hiromu's explanation that he determined to go with his younger brother down to the Bible class at the Adventist mission headquarters in Tokyo's Suginami Ward.

The more Yasushi studied the more he realized that a lot of his life was going to have to be changed. One of his most pressing problems was that of his beloved high school. All Japanese elementary and secondary schools must be attended six days a week—Mondays through Saturdays. What was he to do?

He made inquiries and found out exactly what he expected: The teachers were entirely unsympathetic to any elective absences. He would either have to go to school on Saturdays or leave.

He took his problem to his Bible teacher, and together they took it to their God. Soon strange things began to happen.

About that time there was considerable Communist activity in unsettled postwar Japan. The schools were the chief instruments for this political ideology. And Tokyo High School was no exception.

Yasushi went to the high school one day determined to make an appointment with the principal and either obtain a permit for Sabbath absence or give up his schooling there. He decided this knowing that it would mean the loss of his chance for admission to premedical school the next year. But that day, before he could make his appointment, he noticed that a number of the students were having a mass meeting. It was led by a group of Communist students who were determined that they would go to school only five days a week.

Before the next Sabbath arrived, permission was granted by the faculty of the Tokyo High School granting its students permission to go to school any five days of the week that they selected. Yasushi San knew that his prayer had been answered.

But now in this famed medical school Yasushi was up against an entirely different problem. This time it was not the faculty as a whole, but one determined teacher who was standing in his way.

Despite the fact that he always missed his Sabbath classes, Tamura San stood near the top in his scholarship record. He had been given permission to use the notes of his classmates for Sabbath classes.

But examinations were another matter. This was the first time in his entire medical course that they had come on Sabbath.

At Chiba University a student-faculty committee schedules all examinations—all but the finals. Yasushi had been elected to this committee the first year as the freshman member. Next, he was sophomore representative. Then, junior! Then, senior! God had ever intervened for the faithful lad. As committeeman he had seen to it that his tests were always arranged for week days. But these finals were traditionally scheduled at the individual professor's wish. It was plain that God was testing this young man.

Tamura San and I recalled the experiences of Joseph, Esther, and Daniel. Our hearts were filled with absolute confidence that God would overrule here. So we bowed by the desk and committed our ways to Him, reminding Him of His promises.

There had been less happy stories—the recent one of the young Adventist doctor in south Japan. A fine young doctor, a new Adventist, had gone to his pastor, asking what he should do about his examinations for government license to practice. They had been scheduled on Sabbath. The pastor had said, "God will surely overlook it this once." But how conscience stricken and unsatisfied the new believer had felt after writing his tests on God's day.

"I've already made up my mind," assured Tamura San.

"God bless you, boy," was my reaction.

I counseled him to see his professor once more and promised to write a letter to Dr. Suzuki, the stubborn professor. But it was not likely to be easy. Professors are a law unto themselves in Japan. They are revered. And Professor Suzuki would lose face if he changed his mind now. That would never do. Besides, he had no sympathy whatever for Yasushi's problem.

"Are you crazy?" he had asked.

"No, I don't think so," had been the modest reaction. "But I must obey my God."

"You can't graduate without this examination, and I am not changing it for you or anyone else. *Bakana mane wa yamenasai* ["Don't be a fool"]."

It was with this threat ringing in his ears that Tamura San had come to me. The next morning was Monday. In college chapel just before prayer I shared this experience with the students in a character talk, and asked all to pray.

"We must expect an answer from God before next Sabbath," they were reminded.

I also voiced my certainty that God would answer *before the next Sabbath*.

Both students and teachers were thrilled at the prospect. For they knew well the problems brought by the Sabbath in Japan. And here was a clear-cut situation. Professors just don't change their minds about such things—not in Japan, where loss of face is a very serious matter.

All wondered what was going on in the mind of God— how He would work out this problem. The campus was tense in anticipation, for we all knew that Tamura San was being counted on heavily in the years ahead for our medical work at the Tokyo Sanitarium.

Shortly after the chapel service, I was scheduled to go to Tokyo, some fifty miles away, for a business appointment. Snow was heavy on the ground and it was nearly two miles to the railroad station. For much of the way the bicycle was more of a burden than a help, and I breathed a prayer for help to reach the through train, which would make the appointment. But—

Just as I rode up to the front of the station, the train was chugging out. I felt almost like a bride left waiting at the altar, for it meant an hour's wait for another train, a slow one at that. But then a still, small voice seemed to repeat, "All things work together for good."

At Chiba, where I had to change to the electric train for Tokyo, I was early enough to find a vacant place on one of the long side seats so common in Japanese trains. I sat down and began the work I took to fill the travel time. Soon the crowd filled the train, with most passengers standing, as usual, in the center of the cars.

Just before the doors closed an old Japanese gentleman stumbled in. Elderly, he obviously needed a seat. When I pushed a little and made room, without hesitation he came over to sit down. With a nod of appreciation he went to work on a well-filled appointment book.

A distinguished-appearing man, he intrigued me. So after a few minutes I broke the silence in favor of a pleasant conversation. The weather was cold, we agreed, but the snow was beautiful—a sweet breath of purity. It was easy to look at and easy to talk about. This led our discussion to Christianity, America, Seventh-day Adventists, and Japan Missionary College. He showed by many questions his intense interest in our college plan of balanced education and of Christian social service work.

Soon it became apparent that my new friend was a distinguished gentleman indeed, and possibly a tool of God. "My name," he offered, handing me his engraved card, "is Matsumura." He was Dr. Susumu Matsumura, emeritus professor of public health of Chiba University Medical School!

The still, small voice again spoke to me. "Tell him about Yasushi Tamura."

Dr. Matsumura was greatly interested. "I know Professor Suzuki well," he smiled; "he was a student of mine."

And then he added thoughtfully, "Please let me help you.

We quickly made arrangements for Yasushi to meet him the next day, Tuesday. And then my thoughts burst into words. "Dr. Matsumura, I believe you are the answer to our prayers."

"So *desu ne, so desu ne* ["So it is, so it is, isn't it"]?" he agreed in solemn astonishment. His heart was open. I arranged to send him some books, and reluctantly bade him good-by at his Tokyo destination.

Tuesday morning Tamura San was at Dr. Matsumura's home. The old professor picked up the telephone and called Dr. Suzuki. He told him about the great work of the Seventh-day Adventists, of his "very close friend, Dr. Moore." And then spoke out for Tamura San.

"Send him over in the morning," answered the professor who the morning before had turned down the young medical student in caustic ridicule.

The next morning Tamura San presented himself at Dr. Suzuki's office with mixed feelings.

"Why do you disturb people like this?" was the professor's reaction to the polite bow of the young Adventist. "Do you always go around annoying people?"

Before Tamura San could answer, the professor went on, "As a special favor to my old teacher, Dr. Matsumura, I am changing your examination to Thursday. Now go on, and don't go around bothering people any more."

And on he went, with praise on his lips and a song in his heart, back to my home, where we began counting up blessings: the vindicated faith of a Seventh-day Adventist youth, the aroused interest of a distinguished

Buddhist gentleman, the thrill to our student body of a positive answer to their prayers, a miracle from the hand of God!

For God knew well that the only way the stubborn professor could save his face while changing his mind was for him to bow to the desires of a revered elder teacher. This was an honor to him. And Yasushi was an honor to God.

All the neighboring crops were deep in mud, but every last one of her rice stalks was standing there.

Paddies and Promises

TAKADA SAN had lived long in his adopted land, the American territory of Hawaii. But in all his living he had never lost so much as a thimbleful of his loyalty to *Dai Nippon,* the great Japan motherland. But now there were rumblings of war. They were not so clearly recognized generally, but in the recesses of the Japanese secret society the signs were unmistakable.

"Okasan," he said to his Christian wife one evening after the children had gone to bed, "we must go to Japan. I am getting old, and I must die in the motherland."

Tomie Takada was much younger than her Buddhist husband. She had been used to faithful obedience ever since she had been matched off in the old Japanese manner by a none-too-wise "go-between" some twenty years before.

When she had learned the truth of the Saviour, she had been quick to accept, for it was the only real strength that she had in her life. In return for his tolerance of her faith she would do almost anything for her husband that a faithful wife could rightly do.

"When do we go?" was her only question.

A few months later, with their five sons and one daughter, the Takadas were farming several paddies of rice land in southern Kyushu, Japan's large southern island.

It was a strange life for the children, all of whom were American citizens by virtue of their birth in American territory. But stranger still were the feelings that throbbed in their hearts when a few months later the Japanese War Ministry announced that Japan was at war with America.

"Teach me what Thou wouldst have me to do," was her faithful prayer morning and evening as Tomie Takada gathered her little ones about her. Faithfully she worked their rice paddies, even when her husband was out with the village men, keeping ample company with his bottle of sake, Japan's rice wine.

One by one the children went away to school, studying with mixed feelings the war doctrines of Tojo, the permanent prosperity doctrine of the War Ministry, and the divinity of the Emperor. Relearning their native tongue compounded their problems, but served to build self-discipline.

The angels assigned by Heaven to watch over the little family did their work well, and the little family was safe under the protection of God.

Mr. Takada did not know why his family was being so signally favored while those all about him were losing many of their loved ones. But Tomie Takada's testimony was ever the same when she met her fellow Adventists.

"God has promised that if we pay our tithe and give our hearts to Him that He will rebuke the devourer for our sake, and I believe Him."

It was as simple as that. The terror by night and arrow by day were not of much concern to this dedicated Christian mother.

But just at the end of the war, when Japan was in the great writhing throes of a bitter imperial death, Father Takada died, leaving behind him six lively, intelligent youngsters and their loving, but careworn and work-calloused mother.

Gathering her "gifts of heaven" about her, she planned carefully. She knew it would be a struggle to keep her family alive. But ever the center of her plan was her stewardship, recognition of the One to whom they owed their all. She determined as always to pay her tithe and to present her thank offerings to God.

The two oldest sons soon found jobs. They had voted in Japanese elections at the last of the war so must now stay in Japan. The third and fourth sons returned to American territory as soon as the complicated red tape of repatriation could be unwound. Soon they were in the armed forces, where they were marked by their faithfulness to their mother's God. Now only two children were left with Tomie Takada, and one of them, Yorihiro, her youngest son, was ready for the academy of Japan Missionary College.

"Yorihiro must go to Naraha," Tomie spoke quietly to her little daughter one day.

"Yes, Mother," Etsuko agreed.

"That will mean much work for you and me," the knowing Mother continued.

"Yes, Mother," the little girl loved her mother and wanted to honor her in any way she could.

"This means some sacrificing for you," the voice of the older woman seemed somewhat ominous.

"That's all right, Mother," she agreed.

"Yes, my child, all will be all right as long as we are right with God."

That year Yorihiro went to school. And that year God prospered his mother's three rice paddies more than ever before. In fact, for two years Tomie Takada's three *ta* bore such rich harvests that she was constrained to share a new hope with her little girl.

One evening as they sat on the *tatami* floor about their low table and opened their Bibles for worship, Mrs. Takada's smile had a special twinkle.

"Would you like to go to Naraha next year?" Japan Missionary College was often referred to as Naraha, its nearby railway station.

Etsuko was flabbergasted.

"I really mean it," her mother reassured her.

"Oh, I would be so happy," Etsuko answered. "But what about you?"

"I am willing to leave that up to God, my dear."

Mother and daughter worked harder than ever to make sure that their 1951 crop was the best possible.

"The rest we will leave to God," they agreed.

But the enemy of souls had his eyes on the rice crop too. Just before the rice began to mature, the paddies of the Kagoshima valleys were infested with the dreaded pests.

"We are just reminding you, Father," Mother and daughter prayed that night, "of Thy promise to rebuke the devourer," and despite the warning that the crop would be affected, both Tomie and Etsuko slept the sleep of the righteous that night. They had taken all the measures they could. The rest was up to God.

"What did you use on your rice?" the agricultural experts asked Tomie on their routine check.

"I did just as you suggested," she answered.

"But we mean," they motioned about them, "how do you account for this healthy rice when all around you is infested."

"Why, my God kept the pests away just as He promised He would," was her simple answer.

The frustration of the experts turned to intense interest as she explained the principle of tithe and Christian stewardship.

God must have been watching. Once again He was quite willing to underline His promises, which already stood out in bold relief in Tomie's heart. This time He used one of the worst typhoons in the history of southern Japan.

A few weeks later, on October 14 of the same year, the Takada rice was ripe, with the grain head just falling over— the shy indication of this wholesome plant that it is ready to be harvested. The evening newscast was filled with storm warnings. The big typhoon started near the Philippines, glanced off Okinawa, and was now headed directly for Kagoshima.

"You are warned to tie down your animals and equipment and prepare for the severest blow," the announcer warned. "The typhoon is moving toward Kagoshima at 15 miles an hour with winds up to 160 miles an hour at its center."

That night mother and daughter went to their Master Farmer again, reminding Him of the urgent seriousness of the typhoon.

"Thou hast told us that we should send our children to Christian schools," mother recalled once again, "and we are counting on this crop to send Etsuko to Naraha. We are counting on Thee to rebuke the devourer. But in all, may Thy will be done."

That night Tomie and Etsuko Takada slept far better than their neighbors, but it was nevertheless hard to restrain their excitement as they prepared in the morning to inspect their paddies. Already, outside their door on the washed-out village streets, grief was being expressed in countless ways as the news of the damage and the dead was passed from mouth to mouth.

Tomie and Etsuko looked out across the neighboring *ta* They could see that the golden grain was smashed flat in the flooded paddies. They headed for their own paddies, located some distance from each other, quite a way from the village center.

"Look," cried Etsuko, by far the faster of the two, as she waved her hand to hurry her mother on. "It's standing— high!"

"Thank our wonderful God," was all that Mrs. Takada could say. For all around her little paddy, right up to within six inches of her rice all the neighboring crops were deep in mud, but every last one of her rice stalks was standing there, head tipped politely, smiling its invitation for harvest.

Thrilled and encouraged, off they went to the second paddy. The same experience awaited them there.

After that they hardly needed to go over to the other side of the village to see the third. But, so thrilled that they wondered if they were dreaming, they couldn't wait. Sure enough, the third paddy was standing with as beautiful and courteous a welcome as the first.

"Let's go home and thank Jesus," Etsuko uttered the words just ahead of her mother.

But it wasn't so easy to get home. Their astonished neighbors gathered around them wherever they went.

"Sometimes the wind would blow down the rice in part of the paddy and not in other parts," they acknowledged wide-eyed, "but never did we see anything like this."

"Yes, if it had been just one *tambo,* I might understand," added another neighbor in astonishment, "but all three, and right up the edge of their line! I can't understand it."

Tomie and Etsuko were kept much busier than usual that day, but had little time for harvest. They were testifying of the wonderful power of the promise-keeping God to marveling visitors who came from miles around as word spread like only country gossip can.

The agricultural experts came too. But they were not skeptical any more. The Takada crop was by far the most valuable in the countryside.

Etsuko gave her testimony during the second Friday vesper service of the new academy year. It was easy to understand her belief in the principle of returning to God His own, for God had kept His promises. He had rebuked the devourer and had poured out such a blessing that Etsuko was there to tell of it.

"Come in, friend," he invited, pulling his heavy tanzen closer about him.

The Gambler Takes a Chance

MOTO was a gambler—not a high-lying, suave, society operator, but an ordinary, low-down, alley crook. What was worse, he had married one of his own kind, Teruko, the kind of woman the underworld tags with its own private names. There was no special affection in their relationship. At least it was not evident. Theirs was a partnership in crime—crime against their government, their community, their neighbors, their three children, themselves, and God.

But now for the first time Moto was really shaken. It would have to be something unusual indeed to break down the steel nerve and caustic reserve of this hardened gambler. Even when his best friend "took the rap" and went to jail in his place, he was scarcely turned from his wicked course.

"Sensei, Sensei!" Moto was pounding hard on the door of the *bokushi-kan,* the pastor's little house behind the Kisarazu church. "Sensei, I must see you!"

One evening the year before when their baby was sick he and Teruko, walking the streets in discouragement, had slipped into an evening meeting. They did not know why at the time, but something seemed to push them in. They had studied the Bible for a while with the friendly young minister and his senior pastor, Hokama, but lost interest almost as soon as their little one recovered.

"Who is it?" The weary voice crept from inside the paper-windowed doors and through the shutters.

"It's me—Moto. You remember me, don't you, Sensei?" he answered, half-pleadingly, through the chill night air, "Moto the—the gambler."

"Just a moment." Pastor Watanabe was already down in the *genkan,* the cement-floored entryway, unscrewing the quaint Japanese shutter lock. "Come in, friend," he invited, pulling his heavy *tanzen* closer about him as the cold wind invited itself in along with the gambler.

"My wife has gone, and—and the children too."

By the time he sat down, Moto seemed almost hysterical, strange behavior indeed for him. Further words would not come clearly. Watanabe leaned forward.

"Tell me about it," he suggested quietly, praying silently as he spoke.

The gambler made an effort, but his tongue seemed to be tied in knots.

"Perhaps we should take you home," the young minister ventured, recalling privately the tales of drug addiction and its strange aftereffects. Perhaps Moto had been dosing himself again to keep himself awake and alert on one of his many professional gambling sprees.

"No, no! I know what you are thinking." Fear of losing his last hope for help had restored his speech. "I am not drunk; I am not drugged."

"Then tell me your problem," the pastor invited softly, and waited patiently as the troubled man struggled to collect his wits and regain his composure.

"My wife has left me. She has gone to Aomori. She has taken the children with her. She is expecting another child soon." The sentences were gushing out now. "And she says she is through with me, that even Heaven can't help me."

The gutteral side-mouthed underworld voice was now entirely out of character, almost ready to break. The young minister was thinking deeply, unaware of the cold fingers of the winter night that were trying to reach down his neck and up from his bared ankles. "Perhaps there *is* some natural affection in this poor wreck," he thought, recalling now for the first time some significant actions that night a year before when the sickness of their little child had brought them to his door.

"Now I must go to jail for six months. My trial will be finished soon. Maybe it will be worse."

"Indeed it may well be worse," the pastor thought. Illegal sale of narcotics had become a serious offense in postwar Japan. And his guest was notorious in this traffic.

There were a few moments of silence.

"There is not much we can do tonight, is there, Moto San? And it is very late." He watched his visitor's reactions carefully. "I would like to have you talk with Hokama Sensei tomorrow. We will do all we can to help you."

Watanabe knew that Moto had especially liked the American-Japanese pastor-teacher from Japan Missionary College ever since those studies the year before.

"You think *he* will help me?" There was for the first time a note of hope.

"Yes, *they* will help you. You know Pastor Hokama never works without God." Watanabe now tapped the gambler on his husky chest. "But whether or not you are really helped will depend on your heart."

He nodded thoughtfully. "I have always taken a chance before. What is there to lose?" He took a deep breath. "But I am going to need a lot of praying."

The two silently moved to their knees.

In a northern Japan town of Aomori all was quiet in the ancestral home. In the freezing winter, with unheated homes, the Japanese go to bed with the chickens. Grandmother, Grandfather, their recently returned daughter and her three little ones lay side by side on the *tatami* floor, wrapped well in their *futon*. All were sleeping soundly, all, that is, except Teruko. Her mind would not give her peace.

All that afternoon the children had been asking her about Daddy. And now, lying there flat on her back, she too felt her need for their daddy as she thought of the child soon to be born.

"There must be a better way," a voice kept seeming to say to her. "You can't run away from this." Little did she realize that at this same hour these very words were being spoken to her husband by Pastor Hokama in the little Kisarazu *bokushikan.*

As they sat there, feet folded under them, Asian style, on the rice straw *tatami* floor, the college teacher-pastor was talking sympathetically but frankly with the earnest gambler. Hokama had encountered many problems since taking over this pastorate as a practical part of his college duties.

"We will write Teruko tonight, admit the situation frankly, and do all we can to persuade her to return to you."

" "*Domo,"* Moto smiled and nodded gratefully.

"But you must realize, my friend, that we cannot guarantee you anything unless you give your heart and life to God."

The gambler was visibly stirred.

"I will be happy to see you as often as is necessary in the next few weeks, but I want you to realize that much more depends upon you than upon me."

Carefully the men wrote the letter. Thoughtfully they corrected and redrafted it until finally, with a word of prayer, they sealed it for posting.

A few days later Teruko sent a letter to her uncle in Kisarazu.

"Tell the pastor I am grateful for the help he has offered, but even God cannot help in this situation. I would like to come back, but I have tried it before and this time I know it is hopeless."

The letter told of inner struggle, but ended on a note of finality.

Gathering that night at the midweek prayer service, the little church group made it a matter of prayer. Praying with them that night was the gambler—a gambler who had decided to take a chance with God.

That very hour in Aomori, again lying on her back near the sleeping family at her ancestral home, Teruko could not sleep. A strange voice kept talking to her, reminding her of the counsel given to her by Pastor Hokama months before, telling her again and again that she must not run away from her problem.

Rising silently from under the heavy covers and rearranging them carefully about her youngest child who lay near her, she headed for the low table in the far corner of the house. Closing the sliding door behind her which separated the sleeping room from the rest of the house, she switched on the dim light in front of the closet. Selecting from a lacquered box a sheet of thin writing paper, she knelt beside the little table and began writing. Dipping her pen again and again in the little, near-empty bottle, she wrote swiftly of many things—of the heaviness on her heart, of the strange voice that had been speaking to her night after night.

"But tonight it seems to be telling me in a special way that I must return to you. We will take the train Saturday night. Can you meet us at Ueno station on Sunday morning?"

"Look at this!"

Moto was walking up the church sidewalk Sabbath morning waving a letter to Pastor Hokama and his assistant, Watanabe.

"She is coming back!" He was exuberant.

"Do you know what this means, Moto San?" Hokama asked.

"Yes, it means that God has answered our prayers," he answered enthusiastically.

"Exactly."

"My wife says that if the church is willing to do that much for her family that she must do something too."

Moto moved with the pastors on into church. And there he has been every Sabbath since.

In view of his sentence it was found that he was entitled to a retrial in a higher court. He knew he had been guilty, but was advised to appeal, and a lawyer was found to present his case. During this interval he studied the Bible faithfully and found it to be an anchor to his soul.

The police could not understand the change that had taken place. His life to them had been an open book, with its pages badly soiled. His neighbors marveled at the new Moto, and some were drawn to his church. Even his lawyer was so impressed by his change that he canceled his fee.

Leaving his gambling den, Moto had looked for a respectable business of some kind. Without funds, and unable to obtain a job because of his record, he finally turned to collecting junk—just about the lowest kind of labor there is in Japan. His former friends ridiculed him, pointing out how easy they were living by gambling. But he remained steadfast.

Wherever he would go people noticed his good health and his disposition, and asked him the reason for the change.

"Although I do not have riches any more, I have something far greater," he always testified.

"What do you mean?" they would inevitably ask.

"I have Christ, a Saviour."

Nearly all of his friends predicted that he would be a failure as a junk collector. Most junk men in Japan were dishonest and careless in dealing with their customers. They would take the good junk and leave the rest scattered about. But not so Moto. When shown a pile of junk that he could have or that he could purchase at a low price, he would not only take that which was salable, but he would clean up all the refuse nearby. Soon he became one of the most prosperous junk merchants in the community. The more he prospered, the more his house-to-house testimony continued to lead others to his church.

The old-timers were amazed at his prosperity.

"How do you do it?" they asked. "All the rest of us are having a hard time."

"God is my help," he answered forthrightly. "I talk with Him about my business every day before I leave home, treat my customers fair, and He takes care of the rest."

Soon the people who shunned junk men as low and menial became frank admirers of Kisarazu's new businessman. They were glad to see him come and quick to welcome him back. They admired his religion as a practical one as they saw their yards cleaned up quickly and neatly by the man who had one time been the scourge of their town.

"You never take a chance when you choose Jesus," Moto now tells his friends. And by his testimonies he had won five of them for his Saviour by the time he was baptized. One of them was a gambling crony. Now they agree completely that it is only when a gambler does not choose God that he really takes a chance.

"But our method is different from the ordinary junk men."

Two Wrongs Make It Right

THE sweet strains of the wedding hymn wafted out on the late summer air. It was indeed a mixed multitude that had gathered for the Christian marriage ceremony in the little Adventist church. Now and then a passer-by would stop and listen. Occasionally one would turn in. But only a few people were aware of the story that was reaching its climax in the Kisarazu chapel that Sunday afternoon.

Ota San had been born the eldest son in a strong Buddhist home. A popular and likable boy, his family was quick to extend him all the privileges of the first born, and more. Here they made their mistake, for Ota proved quick to take advantage of his family and friends.

"Son," his mother approached him one day, "have you been needing money lately?"

"Why do you ask me such a question?" Ota evaded.

"Just tell me, son," she answered quietly.

"What if I did?"

"I was just wondering."

After that his mother and father were more careful about where they left their money, but were also careful not to cross their willful son.

"Where is my suit?" queried his father one day as he was preparing for a formal village occasion. "Does anyone know where my suit is?"

"It should be right there in the *oshiire*," his wife answered quickly, and obediently proceeded to show him.

But the suit was not there. Nor was his hat. Nor was her kimono. Nor her best *obi*, the all-important waist decoration for the Japanese woman's formal attire.

The children were questioned, but nobody seemed to know. Sensing that a thief had been in the house, they reported the theft to the police.

A quick check by the ever-efficient detective officer placed the offense squarely at the doorstep of Ota San. The grief-stricken parents did all they could to shield him, but it made no impression on the cool police or the stern judge. He must go to prison.

By this time Ota was a confirmed gambler. And it seemed that he was not always successful. After his release from prison he was caught once more and sent away. And again this happened.

"He really doesn't seem to be the bad type," the judge wrote in his decision, "but when he gets into bad company he cannot resist temptation."

This time his parents decided that they had borne with him long enough, and finally cut him off from the family.

One black day he was arrested for dealing in drugs and was sharply questioned by the police. It turned out that it was not Ota San but his close friend, Moto, who was to be blamed this time.

But Moto had to be protected, Ota thought, because he had a wife and three children.

"Your honor," Ota addressed the judge. "Your honor, I should like to go to prison in the place of my friend."

"What?" the judge was incredulous. "This from you?"

"Yes, let me take the place of Moto. I have no family, no children, and I am cut off from my home."

"I will study this case and let you know tomorrow."

The next morning Ota San was called to the judgment bar in place of his friend.

"Ota, I have studied this case carefully. In the place of your friend I sentence you to six months in prison." The judge was hopeful for the effect on Moto.

Later that month a turn of events came into Moto's life that eventually led him to become a Christian. Deeply involved in his own personal difficulties, he seldom found time to meet with his friend in the faraway prison.

When, six months later, the time came for Ota San's release, Moto was there to greet him and take him to his now untroubled Christian home.

"What has come over this place?" Ota gestured with a sweep of his hands, eyes wide open.

"Come on in," Moto invited happily, "and see for yourself."

After the traditional Japanese greetings all sat around on the *tatami* in the sunny southern room. Everything about the house was neat and clean, and for some strange reason the Shinto altar and Buddhist gods were absent from their usual recesses.

"There is something different about this place, I tell you," Ota insisted.

"Do you like it?" his host questioned.

"Can't say but that I do," he replied, still looking at Moto questioningly.

"Teruko and I have found Jesus."

Ota looked troubled.

"You see we are Christians now."

Moto San enthusiastically told the story of his conversion.

"If you are really telling the truth, I would like to hear more about a religion like that," Ota remarked thoughtfully.

"Christ is a little bit like you," Moto averred, praying for the right words. "He gave His life that we might be saved, just like you gave yourself in prison that I might be free." Ota San didn't understand completely, but somehow the news had the sweetest sound that he had heard in a long time.

For weeks he studied earnestly with Moto and his pastor.

Ota's father was now dead, but soon his mother received word that the son who had disgraced her family was now an upright man.

"I cannot believe the reports I hear," she wrote to her Kisarazu friends. "Only a miracle can change my son, and since the great war I have lost faith in miracles."

Her friend wrote back immediately. "Yes, in the war our gods let us down. But Ota is changed, even if it has to be a miracle."

"Send him to see me," she finally wrote; "I must see for myself."

Whenever her son had previously appeared at her door she had known that he was up to no good, and this time her heart was gripped by the same old fear.

"I will test him," she determined silently.

Coldly she received him, keeping her distance. No matter how thoughtfully and cordially he spoke she seemed hardened to him. She tried him well.

Ordering him about the house to do menial tasks that she normally did herself, ever cautious not to give any evidence of the affection that lingered in her heart, she tested him again and again. But within the hour, like Joseph, she could hold her feelings no longer. The old mother broke down and wept on the chest of her long-lost son.

"Now I know that what I have heard is true. I had lost an evil son, but the one I have found is good."

One day, after Ota had joined his friend, Moto, in the junk business, they were cheerfully making the rounds of their clients. Today they were going to try a new place.

"We will give you the best price—" the men began.

"I'll take care of my own junk," came the rude answer.

"But our method is a bit different from the ordinary junk men," Moto protested mildly, and then gave a clear testimony of his religion and of what God had done for him.

A woman employee stopped and listened for a moment to the strange recital.

"That is a wonderful story indeed," she thought, and waited until the men were through. She then approached the two cautiously.

"I am sorry that he talked to you that way," she said. "Is it really true—all that you told him?"

"It is more true than we even said," Ota San replied. "Why don't you come to our church and find out for yourself?"

The next Sabbath Kimiko was in church, and never missed a Sabbath after that.

But after her first day in church she had to return to her place of employment, which was also her home.

"I have a special job for you, Kimiko," her employer called to her. Kimiko obediently listened, but what she heard did not sound good to her—it sounded so different from what she had heard in church that very morning. Even in her disgraceful place of business the thing that her employer was asking her now seemed to her dishonest.

Kimiko had been born into a poor family, so poor that at fourteen she had been sold to a brothel and there had lived a life of misery for more than ten years. She was not her own. She had been bought by a householder and was his slave to do anything he commanded.

But the next day she had no peace. Before this she had not thought too much about complying with such a vile order, but this time it was different. She had gone to God's church and now what she had done bothered her conscience all night, so much indeed that she went to the man she had wronged and confessed. The surprised client assured her of his forgiveness. Her employer was amazed when the matter was reported to him.

"What is going on here?" her employer demanded after summoning her into his room.

"I did not go to God's church before," she replied meekly.

"What do you mean 'God's church'?"

"The Christian church over there," she said, motioning to the east.

"Do you realize that you are my property and you will do as I say?" her proprietor demanded heatedly.

Kimiko did not answer. She was coming to realize that she could not continue her work there and still go to God's church. A few days later she made an appointment with Pastor Hokama.

"I have a little money saved," she told the pastor. "But not quite enough to buy myself away from him. He always keeps his girls in debt, and no matter how much we try we are never free."

"How much do you need?" the pastor asked kindly.

"It will take four thousand yen more," Kimiko replied reticently, voice quivering, for she realized that four thousand yen was nearly half a month's salary for the average Japanese, and the raising of that amount seemed virtually impossible.

"God will find a way," Pastor Hokama assured her. "After all, your debts are much lower than those of most of the girls."

The church members got together, and before the week was over the full ransom was placed in the hand of the unhappy proprietor. Kimiko was free! Earnestly she studied about the Saviour who had given Himself a ransom for her.

"He must be a lot like you," she told Mrs. Hirose, her Bible instructor.

"No, we just want to be like Him," she replied, "and you can be too."

After several months of Bible studies from Mrs. Hirose, a strong lay worker, and her husband, Kimiko was enrolled in the baptismal class. There she met again the man who had first encouraged her to find Christ. It was Ota, the gambler and thief who had once been a scourge in Kisarazu.

Now they were being joined in one of the sweetest weddings the world will ever see. Its beauty was not in a lovely bridal gown, for her kimono was plain. Nor was it a cutaway coat on the groom. He was dressed simply, in a borrowed suit. It was the love of Christ that shone through both bride and groom; it was the radiant face of Moto, the best man, and the tender happiness of the matron of honor, Mrs. Hirose.

A gambler who had given his heart to Christ was wed to a modem Mary Magdalene, now a princess of God. Two wrongs had been made right in Jesus.

"Japan Missionary College?" he asked, surprised but obviously pleased. "Do you know my friend, Dr. Moore?"

Fumio San

IT was an unfriendly night in late 1951. It seemed as if the biting north wind were trying to blow the rain like little bullets right through us. We waited shivering on Yokohama's long South Pier.

"Will that launch ever come?" Hartley Ludden queried doubtfully, his breath blowing vapor streams in the early winter air.

The little boat was to take us out to bring the missionaries' baggage from the ship that had just brought them in.

While we were waiting, huddled under a *kasa*—a Japanese oilpaper umbrella—a boy in uniform stepped up and spoke in hesitant English.

"Won't you come to my house?" he invited, motioning to the little gate shack in the center of the pier.

"Gladly," we gratefully answered, stepping quickly over and inside.

Our host was Fumio Takei, a customs guard on the Great Pier. Fumio was only eighteen years of age, obviously new at his business, and possibly for this reason much friendlier than many of the customs guards we had come to know.

For an eighteen-year-old who had not yet had an opportunity for college education, Fumio San had learned his English well. His big friendly smile and his sincere courtesy were a contrast with some customs officers we had known. From force of habit I reached into my coat pocket and pulled out an enrollment blank for the Voice of Prophecy Bible Course.

"Oh, are you a Christian?" he asked, glancing at the little blue and white sheet.

"That's right."

"I have heard much about Christianity, but I have never had a chance to study it," he mused, slipping into Japanese toward the last.

"This is one of the best Bible courses in the world, and it will not cost you anything," I offered, stepping out of the shelter briefly as I thought I heard the launch. "Just write your name and address, and it will be sent to you right away."

"*Sayonara.*" Moving toward the door, we bade him a grateful good-by.

The chug-chug of the launch motor was coming close now.

The next day, before sending in the enrollment blank, I took Fumio's address and sent him some other literature. But that was the last I heard of him for some time.

The Occupation had ended, and customs restrictions were becoming increasingly difficult not only for the businessmen but also for missionaries. Foreigners soon learn to have a deep respect for these regulations. Apparently many people had abused the privileges. The Japanese Government was tightening down.

A number of missionaries were scheduled to join our mission family in a short period of time that summer of 1953. We knew that they would be bringing along many things that could be subject to high customs taxes and import duties. The Japanese customs laws were so written as to allow considerable latitude on the part of the customs officials, and *a lot depended upon the officer assigned to each case.* Our mission family made this a subject of special prayer, for unfavorable customs levies can cost our missions many thousands of dollars, and the college was in no position to pay anything like that.

The first missionary family to arrive that summer was the Arakakis, an American-Japanese family from California and Hawaii, who had come to join our theology staff at the college. We went down to the port to meet them. It was a happy meeting—both for the newcomers and for the missionaries, who had waited in anticipation for their help and comradeship.

But the customs problem weighed more heavily than usual on us that day. We had been warned that the Japanese customs officers would be more severe on the Japanese-Americans than on the rest of us. It was a jittery wait for the immigration clearance and for the Arakakis to complete their customs declaration forms.

Finally the first load of their baggage came off the ship. Hauled by the Japan Express men from the pier over to the customs office, we followed it like little puppies behind their mother dog, always eager but never sure.

The fidgety wait ended suddenly when from behind us the customs officer stepped briskly, with firm demeanor, over to the Arakakis' luggage. A picture of efficiency, he courteously but impersonally beckoned for his assistants to come with hammers and crowbars to open up the crates and the boxes.

"Mr. Arakaki?" he questioned as he checked the declaration papers.
"That's right."

"Please open your suitcases first," he requested in his clipped Japanese-English, gesturing toward the stack of luggage.

"What are we in for?" we asked ourselves, for this was only the beginning of the personal luggage. The larger part of the freight and baggage items were yet to come from the hold of the ship.

"Over there," he motioned to his "wrecking crew," who knew well how to open boxes and crates posthaste.

"Do you have any cigarettes, liquors?" he started out in his routine questioning of the new immigrants, head down, intent on his business.

"No, we neither smoke nor drink," Arakaki answered.

Several similar questions followed in quick succession.

"Oh, are you missionaries?" he finally asked, after being impressed that there was something different about these people.

"Yes, we are," was the reply. Shigenobu Arakaki had already told him this at first, but the young officer had been too preoccupied to hear.

"What kind of work will you do?" he continued his quizzing.

"I am a teacher, a Bible teacher," was the patient response.

"Where are you going to teach?"

"At *San Iku Gakuin* [Japan Missionary College] right over there across the bay," the new teacher replied, gesturing eastward.

"Japan Missionary College?" he asked, surprised but obviously pleased. "Do you know my friend, Dr. Moore?"

"Dr. Moore?" Arakaki questioned in surprise. "Why, he is right here."

With that the young officer looked up for the first time into my face. He was Fumio San, the thoughtful freshman officer we had met that cold, rainy night at South Pier two years before. "We-e-ell, Dr. Moore, I am so *gla-a-a-d* to see you," he enthused, losing himself immediately in reminiscence. "You know, I finished that Voice of Prophecy course!"

"Good!" I was just as enthusiastic.

"And I received a diploma too."

The electricity in the atmosphere was suddenly gone. The warmth was now of another kind. And as he continued the conversation he shut the suitcases, dismissed his helpers, rhythmically stamping the tags on all of the parcels, suitcases, crates, and boxes as fast as he could bring his rubber stamp back and forth from his ink pad to the shipping tags.

A few days later, with all of the dozens of baggage items passed by customs, we looked up Fumio San again. This time it was about the freight from the ship's hold.

"We have a whole truckload of freight for Mr. Arakaki coming in tomorrow," I spoke with some hesitation, but always hopeful. "They will not be unloading the hold baggage tonight, so I will have to wait."

"Well, I will not be on duty tomorrow," Fumio replied, "but if you have the express company bring it in from the boat directly the next day, I will take care of it," he assured us.

Because of weather problems the ship was delayed in unloading and it was easy for us to comply. So, on the appointed day, we returned to Yokohama to escort the big truckload of precious freight from the ship's side to the customs house. Sure enough, Fumio San was there.

We made ready to unload so that he could stamp the boxes freely. We knew well the standard procedure—every box had to be stamped.

"Just a minute," Fumio San raised his hand. "May I see the declaration for this load?" his voice was well modulated but businesslike.

"Yes, here it is." We handed him the green sheet.

"Actually I should stamp all of these boxes," he said, "but I know you, and besides you have a long way to go. It will take us a long time to unload and reload this truck." So saying, he stamped the green sheet—passing the entire load of baggage without an opened slat or a question.

We restrained ourselves from bowing to our knees on the spot, but breathed silent prayers of gratitude.

A few months later, in October of the same year, the experience was repeated when Elder and Mrs. Thomas Blincoe came to head the theology department of the college.

The customs house was a house of profanity. Disappointed businessmen and visitors watched while freight, baggage, and personal effects were thrown about—like the dirt behind a dog in frantic search for a mole. But through all this commotion God silently watched His own. Without question or hesitation the truckloads of baggage and freight for the missionaries and for the mission were stamped clear while all about us were boxes and crates torn apart by the eager assistants.

"I would like to go to your school," Fumio told me quietly one day a few months later.

"How did you happen to decide that?" I was surprised, because I had suggested this a number of times, but always without response.

"I just don't like this kind of business I am in," he replied soulfully. "I am always required to doubt people, and I just don't like to doubt."

Fumio San began to make plans to attend Japan Missionary College.

The sequel to this story is not yet written. Some of the missionaries expressed the fear that the next inspector might not be so considerate. But such concerns they are happy to leave in the hands of God. For, wonder of wonders, our God can even work in the heart of a keen Buddhist youth to make him efficient in forwarding the work of Christian missions.

The girls were castigated both publicly and privately. Every home in Okinawa was filled with the talk of the "strange treasonous sect."

God Turns the Battle

THERE was trouble in the Ryukyus. The battle was just as serious and hard fought as any during World War II, when Adventist youth became famous for the lives they saved. Only this time it was a battle for men's souls.

It centered on the big island of Okinawa.

For the first time the army of God was invading that stronghold of the enemy. Although His strategy was carefully planned, the enemy was vicious in retreat—there were booby traps almost everywhere.

Mr. Yahiku, a conscientious layman from Hawaii, had volunteered for service, and had left home and family to go to Okinawa to join forces with the Jensens, our first missionaries there. Their fiercest competition, surprisingly enough, came from the members of a prominent Protestant church. The key worker in this antagonistic company was a woman, Mrs. Tsukayama.

Our Adventist workers did not know just how to proceed. The people of the island, steeped in ancestor worship, were completely hostile to any kind of religion that held that the "dead know not any thing," and taught the second coming of the Saviour called Christ. The island itself was controlled by a cool, impartial American Army.

They took the only course that any true missionary would take under the circumstances: They sought the counsel of their General.

As usually happens, God had looked ahead generations before. Mrs. Tsukayama, it turned out, was a relative of Mr. Yahiku's. Although definitely unfriendly to our message, this zealous Protestant worker seemed nevertheless a sterling Christian, a hard-working evangelist. As Yahiku San gave her opportunity to tell him of her faith, it became as convenient as the arm on a rocking chair to ask a few mild questions himself. Some of these questions Mrs. Tsukayama could not answer.

Next came the test. Was Mrs. Tsukayama really open for the truth or not? If she was, he knew that she would become an Adventist.

And so she did—but not without a fight from other members of her congregation.

"You don't know what you're doing!" they chorused.

"Are you crazy—joining a minority sect like that?" others exclaimed.

After all she was their most effective worker. Thus they waited upon her almost daily for weeks and months. But she was searching steadfastly. Little by little as she thought it through she realized that she would be compelled to step out.

"I have found the truth!" she finally answered them happily but firmly. And therein lies a beautiful story of a chain reaction that is spreading the third angel's message throughout the entire Ryukyu nation.

With Mrs. Tsukayama in the fold the picture looked much brighter, but God knew even better than our workers that the Sabbath message would be a hard one to be accepted on Okinawa. He knew that the people had to work like ants to eke their living out of the stingy earth. He knew that there if a man did not work seven days a week they think him a sluggard, and what is lower than a sluggard on Okinawa?

Nor were the children exempt, for, as in Japan, every student must go to school six days a week—every day but Sunday—or be expelled. If they do not go, teachers, parents, and other students say that they are lazy and do not love their country. This is a fearful thing in the patriarchal system of Okinawa.

"God, teach us how!" the little company prayed. "Place a feeling of need in the hearts of the people."

Knowing well that one of the best ways to approach the hearts of the people is to help their bodies, Mrs. Tsukayama began with the sick. At the Kin Tuberculosis Sanatorium, in the northern part of the big island, she was welcomed by patients who were glad to have anybody come and help them pass their dreary days. But especially were they delighted with one who had a smile like Mrs. Tsukayama's, a voice so tender, a message so full of hope.

"How are you, dear?" she would greet them. And soon hearts would open.

The first response came from Fuji Miyagi, whose enthusiasm proved contagious. And her close friend, Yasuko Taira, soon followed her example.

"If this Christ is like these people, we must learn to know Him," the girls agreed.

After but a few months of precious study together, Yasuko was transferred to the Itoman Sanatorium, many miles to the south. The enemy thought that he was dividing the camp of God. But he did not realize that, like cells of life, they were dividing to multiply. Fuji and Yasuko became active missionaries in their two hospitals, and the more they shared their new message with others the better they felt. Before long both of them were on their feet and released from the hospital.

The two dedicated young lay workers soon were conducting Bible studies at several homes in northern Okinawa in the towns of Hentona, Okuma, and Kijioka. Skepticism, like a clinging spider's web, met them wherever they traveled. But their prayers were answered as they watched how God had prepared the hearts of the earnest, hard-working people who had been so fiercely set back, their land torn from under them by the last terrible battles of World War II.

They soon were the talk—if not always the toast—of the towns.

One by one, old and young, rich and poor, influential and average, took hold of the faith of God. The first year five young people came to Japan Missionary College from that big island. The second year ten, and the third year twenty. Even the treasurer of the Kijioka township, one of the most influential men in the community, held out against the chiding of his fellow townsmen, and sent his daughter to our Tokyo Sanitarium to become a Christian nurse.

The day of God had dawned on Okinawa.

But the battle had just begun. Any clever enemy is not at all hesitant to prepare his plans before the dawn, and thus the enemy of souls was there with all of his devices.

He had reason to be worried—especially about the young people in the northern villages of the big island who were fast becoming interested in our faith. A number of them were attending the weekly meetings taught by Mrs. Tsukayama and her helpers. The young people were willing to do anything to better the heritage that had been left them by the war. If there was something that was to be offered them by Christianity they wanted it, and badly. But they had failed to reckon with their high school teachers!

In Okinawa, as elsewhere in the Orient, the sensei, or teacher, is held in reverence by everyone from small child to government leader. When he speaks, he is listened to. When he gives instruction, he expects to be obeyed.

Hadn't the young people been told by their Bible teachers at the Kijioka and Okuma meeting that God had commanded them to rest from their work and do good things for their neighbors on the seventh day,

His Sabbath? If that was so, how could they go to school? It was a hard question.

The teachers called each in separately.

"Where have you been these three Saturdays?" they demanded of each.

"At the Christian Bible school," they answered levelly.

"What do you mean by disobeying your teachers this way?" was the next angry question.

"We have learned that we must first obey God," was the firm but humble reply.

This was serious. They were taken before the principal.

The principal at first appealed to them carefully and kindly. He gave special attention to the Tamaki sisters, Toshiko and Yoshiko, and for good reason: They were the honor students of the school.

Looking at Toshiko, he challenged her, "Don't you realize that you are soon to represent our school at the *Undokai* [Okinawa's annual sports festival]?"

Turning to Yoshiko San, he said pointedly, "You are the valedictorian and leader of your class. Surely you will not continue to disgrace your ancestors by an example like this!"

The girls were steadfast. "But we have learned of the true God!" they testified.

"Do you deny the gods of your ancestors?" The principal was becoming heated.

Not being able to make headway by kindness, and fearing the loss of his school's prestige in both scholarship and the all-important festival, the principal became angry and resorted to threat.

"We will refer this to the superintendent of schools and the town council. Your family will be disgraced!"

Administrators in other high schools followed suit. The matter was presented to the superintendent. And soon the Okinawa pot began to boil.

They made no further progress than before. The two maidens and their friends stood firm.

Now, joined by bitter parents, the educators went to the town councils.

Some of the children were beaten. Two were threatened with death. And some gave in. But not Toshiko, nor Yoshiko, nor a number of their friends.

Next the heads of the schools were brought together at the central Okuma office of Mr. Miyagi, the superintendent. There a combined meeting of educators, parents, and town leaders was held. In full cooperation was Mrs. Miyagi, leader of the federated women's clubs of northern Okinawa, a woman who knew her power and wielded it well.

Reporters of the main Okinawa papers were brought in and given colored accounts of the recent happenings. Newspapers are potent on Okinawa, for nearly every island family is a reader. The pot was boiling over.

The next day almost every home in Okinawa was filled with the talk of the "strange treasonous sect" that was making inroads into northern Okinawa and attacking the "very heart of our civilization"—its youth.

Furthermore, it was undermining the foundation of their most sacred beliefs—the divinity of their ancestors. This to them was truly a terrible thing, for the Ryukyuans work all their lives to build their elaborate masonry tombs for death, even though they may own only thatched huts in life. In these tombs elaborate ceremonies are held to ensure the right kind of divinity for the dead.

The girls were castigated both publicly and privately.

"You are disgracing your school and your town," they were shamed.

"You should go to a mental hospital," others cried.

Some still clung to the hope that softness would break them and organized student committees to plead with them.

"Just for the *Undokai!*"

The faithful girls told their story again and again.

"But it would have been more effective recited to a rock," they thought.

Our workers visited the newspaper editors to make the story clear. But the scandal-loving reporters had a strong influence on the editors. The adverse news coverage continued to flare.

"At least you are getting a lot of high-priced publicity awfully cheap," was the comment of the friendly town treasurer to Mrs. Tsukayama one day. But that was scant comfort then.

The American Civil Government offered to step in and order them to allow the young women freedom from school on those days. But our missionaries felt that this was no affair for an occupying force. Their main appeal must go to God.

Then in their extremity God once more began to reveal His plan.

There was also another Yoshiko in Okinawa. But she was not a Christian. This Yoshiko had been seriously injured in the war. The hope of her parents that time would heal her had been mocked at by their gods.

"You must go to Japan," her doctor advised with finality. "You must go to specialists who cannot be found on Okinawa."

Most young Ryukyuans would be excited at the prospect of going to the great home country to the north. But not so with Yoshiko. Not only did she have forebodings of a lengthy and painful hospital experience, but as a much-loved teacher she was also devoted to her highly successful junior high school classes.

Lonely and fearful, upon her arrival in Tokyo she set about to find her former chum and childhood friend, Nobuko, who might be a comfort to her in her days of confinement. Nobuko had come from Okinawa two years before to attend Japan Missionary College.

No sooner had she arrived at the tailored campus outside Tokyo than Yoshiko became lost in reminiscence with her old friend. She postponed her medical appointment as, like fog in new sunshine, preoccupation with her troubles began to disappear. Day by day she lived in fellowship with her Christian friend, walked the closely clipped lawns of the campus, and joined Nobuko at study and work.

"Nobu-chan," she addressed her companion one day in the endearing Asian way. "Nobu-chan, I must come to this college too."

"A wonderful idea," Nobuko enthused. This was just what she had been praying for.

"After all," Yoshiko continued, "I have been teaching for ten years and need a refresher anyway. I will write to my parents today."

Her parents, happy with their daughter's new and brighter outlook, expressed delight with her plan.

One day the two young women went to Tokyo, where Yoshiko was, for the first time, to visit the mission headquarters and the Voice of Prophecy. As she made her way through offices, studios, and clinic, certain memories began to take shape in Yoshiko's mind. Then with strange suddenness she realized that this was the headquarters of the church that had given her father so much trouble. This was the people newspapers of Okinawa had described in such vindictive terms. For Yoshiko Miyagi was the daughter of the superintendent of schools of northern Okinawa.

But by now Yoshiko's heart had been won. She was a devoted student of the Bible and determined all the more to apply for entrance to Japan Missionary College.

She wrote her parents more of her experience. She pointed out the truths and the hopes of her new belief and what it was doing for her mentally and physically. She urged them to inquire of the mission leaders in Okinawa.

This was a strange suggestion to make to Superintendent Miyagi. But in the Orient, parents honor their children even as children honor their parents. And this church was doing something for his daughter that she had needed for many years.

Mrs. Miyagi soon made it a point to visit the Bible studies that she and her husband a few weeks before had condemned publicly. Only this time her heart was open, and with prejudice gone she drank in the gospel news. Mr. Miyagi soon joined her, and before long had invited a Bible worker to give special studies to his family.

"What's doing on that Adventist sect at Okuma?" the editor of the Okinawa *Times* asked his reporter one day. "Stick to that beat!" he warned.

"But the beat's all off," the reporter answered. "We can't dig up a thing!"

The "strange treasonous sect" had suddenly become respectable. Unfavorable discussions were no longer held among the women's clubs of the towns. And interestingly, too, complaints stopped coming from principals and teachers of the high schools. Some of the parents, yet affected by the earlier disturbances, were still unreasonable, but the noise and the shouting gradually died away.

The town treasurer's estimate had been about right. Ours was by far the best-known Christian church now. Hundreds came to rallies where before there had been but few.

The chapter on Okinawa is not yet closed, however, nor will it be until the Saviour comes. But the Miyagi story had been written, and with its writing the work began to blossom like California poppies on a barren mountainside.

Seldom indeed had anything but gossip gone so fast in the Orient.

Mrs. Miyagi began to use her influence in her women's clubs for this "helpful new people who are among us." She made arrangements to send her other daughter north to Japan Missionary College. Mrs. Tsukayama and her helpers became honored guests. The way has opened for the establishment of an Adventist junior academy, and birth was given to unanswerable demands for more workers.

God had turned the battle on Okinawa.

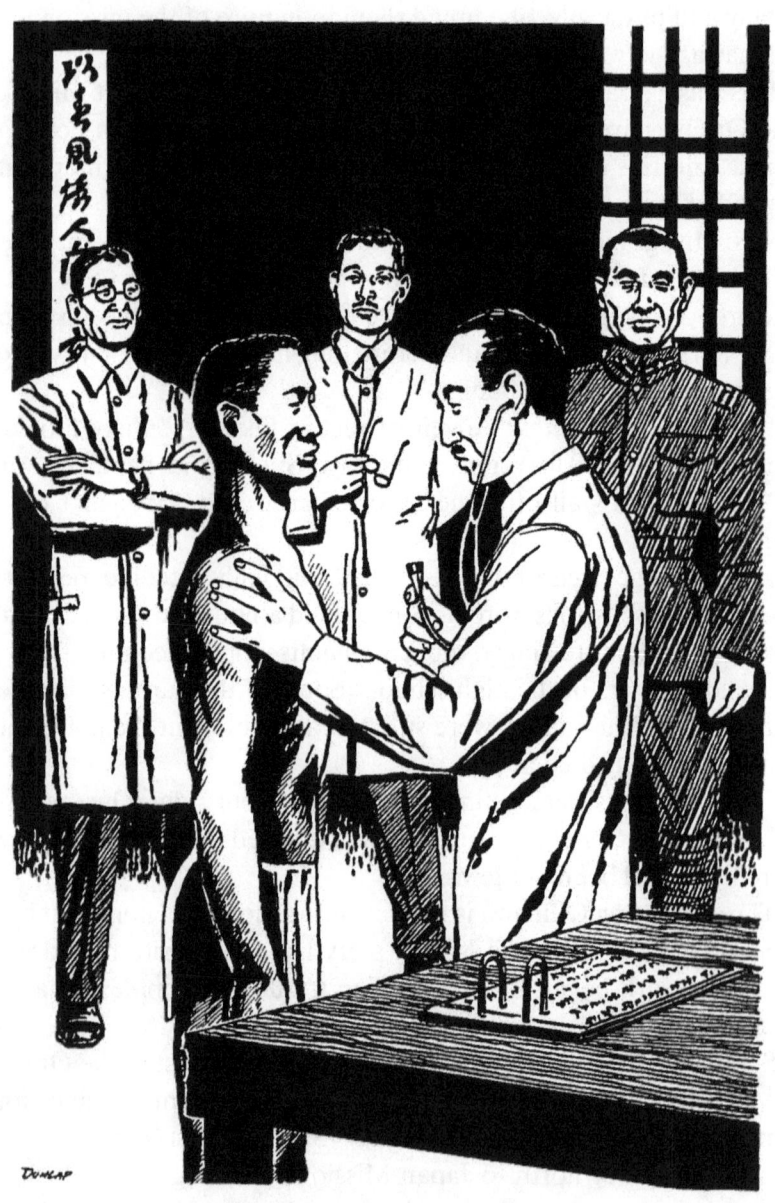

One by one the doctors examined him.

Adventures of a Scientist

IN THE mid 1930's there was excitement among astrophysicists, that elite circle of astronomers who are known as the "mathematicians of the stars." A youthful Japanese genius, a doctoral student at the famed Imperial University, had just developed a new method to determine the composition of stellar objects. The news spread through professional literature all over the world and found its way into great libraries, among them the Library of Congress in Washington, D.C.

But behind this achievement of international recognition an even more important story was being sketched on the records of heaven. For this youth, the son of one of Japan's powerful businessmen, had turned his back on tempting and profitable invitations of Japan's *Zaibatsu,* to give himself in sincere service to the King of the universe, whose planets he held in such awe. This young man was Toshio Yamagata.

During those gray prewar years the young scientist was well aware that as a Christian his every movement was being watched. It was well known among his colleagues that he was a Christian, and, therefore, that he placed God before the Emperor.

About this time he became a professor in a prominent university and also taught in the Adventist girls' school in Tokyo. Before long he was made principal of the school.

Now he was watched more closely than ever, for this school was under special surveillance. And his professorship at Hosei University did not help him any.

Then came July, 1939. The *akagami* (red paper), a greeting from the Emperor, was presented at his door. Yamagata was to have the honor of the Emperor's invitation to serve His Imperial Majesty in the grand army of the Land of the Rising Sun.

What a privilege that is to the average Japanese youth, who reveres the Emperor as God. But to the young educator it was anything but a thrill, for he knew that if he was to be a conscientious Sabbathkeeper in the Japanese Army, it would mean imprisonment or death.

"God, give me power to follow Thee," he prayed. "Thou hast promised that Thou wilt not suffer me to be tempted above that I am able, but will with the temptation make a way to escape, that I will be able to bear it."

With mixed emotions Yamagata himself wondered about his ability to stand. He had seen several young Adventist men drafted and had watched their faith and courage fail. Even the sky seemed that day to weep for the lovely young bride he had taken but a month before.

While awaiting processing and his final call, one day he was reading from *Thoughts From the Mount of Blessing,* where he read again, "If we commit ourselves to God, we have the assurance, 'He will not suffer you to be tempted above that ye are able; but ... .'"

His purpose was crystallized. He was committed. He was not going to worry about what was before him.

After a heart-strangling wait the day for physical examination finally came. Sad farewells were said and the long train trip was made to the examination point in Kyushu, Japan's southernmost island. Recognizing the serious loss to the school, both students and remaining teachers joined in a deep, almost desperate, fellowship of prayer.

Down in a Kyushu barracks room the recruits stood stripped and sweating on that hot July afternoon in 1939. Head shaved, tired from the long trip, the young Adventist teacher gave the appearance of anything but the refined Christian gentleman his friends knew. "Just like a sheep led to the slaughter, I felt that day," he remarked later.

One by one the doctors examined him, six of them. Mechanically they prodded him, ordered him up, ordered him down, turned him around, bent him over, exercised him, opened his mouth, and pushed him on. They made it evident that their job was just as distasteful to them as it was to him. He had been passed by six of the physicians. To Yamagata the picture became as dark as a new-moon night.

Now, stepping before the seventh and final member of the medical team, the naked, newly bald recruit was anything but a man of distinction—at least that is what he thought. But for some reason the medical captain took a closer look at Yamagata's examination form.

Suddenly his officious, mechanical demeanor changed to one of awakened interest.

"Are you a graduate of Meizen Middle School?"

"Yes." The green recruit feared to say more.

"Do you know Mr. Tokunaga?"

"Yes," and taking more courage now at the blossoming friendliness of his examiner, "he was my intimate friend."

The doctor smiled reminiscently. "He used to be very nice to me." And then added regretfully, "You know, Mr. Tokunaga died in China last year in the war."

The gray news was but a momentary prelude to a happy conversation carried on oblivious to the frightened, unhappy line and six impatient but resigned doctors.

Then, taking his pen, the captain looked once more at the record, and in a half-whisper spoke confidentially. "Men of your qualifications are too valuable for cannon fodder. You had better go back home this time. I will fix it up. . . ."

Yamagata was so surprised that he did not even catch the last words of the doctor. He stepped gingerly out of the room, not daring to show his exuberance, but still wondering whether it was all a dream.

When he returned to the barracks, he found that the rest of the recruits were being shipped to Nomonhan on the border of Manchuria, where Russia and Japan were having trouble. Out at the gate of the reservation he found his faithful mother and his bride, who were still earnestly praying and who assured him that all the teachers and girls at the Tokyo school were also together in the covenant of prayer.

The return trip to Tokyo was one of the world's happiest honeymoons.

The young professor was a spectacle to both colleagues and students when he appeared in class with the top of his head nearly as smooth as his face. But the recent haircut was truly forgotten, and knees once more bowed in thanksgiving when it was reported a short while later that the outfit that had gone to Nomonhan was completely wiped out by the Russians.

Later a note came to his home through the city office advising his family that he had been killed in war. "I do not know how it happened," he told his friends later, "but I know that God preserved me and gave me greater strength for things to come."

About four years later, in the early morning of September 20, 1943, several policemen surrounded the Yamagata home. This was common procedure in Japan, and many a citizen under such circumstances either tried to escape or committed hara-kiri when faced with the prospect of arrest.

One of the officers knocked on the door.

Responding quickly and politely, the young professor was courteously handed a warrant of arrest.

"I was just about to eat," Yamagata offered, attempting to maintain his composure.

With much the same gesture as is often granted to one condemned, just before he is executed, the policeman honored Yamagata's request to wait while he ate his breakfast. Shortly afterward he joined them in the big police van and was escorted with a variety of other citizens to the Tokyo Metropolitan Police Station. There, without further questioning, he was thrust into a dark, dungeonlike cell whose wrought-iron decoration gave him little comfort.

Later in the day he was called before the chief of the religious section of the thought-control police. One by one the chief recited the steps ahead of him if he should continue his present beliefs. Name by name the list of workers and leading members of the church was read, and the police's plan for each one.

"You are charged," the chief read firmly, "with foolishly worshiping your God before the Emperor. And furthermore," he continued, "with belief in a cataclysmic change of the world, which you admit is not consistent with the permanent-prosperity doctrine of our nation."

The young professor knew well that the second charge was in many respects just as important as the first one, for the "permanent prosperity" theory was one of the guiding principles of the war.

His beliefs virtually amounted to treason.

"What is your answer?" the chief demanded.

"I must say the same as before," Yamagata replied kindly but firmly, knowing that further explanations would only antagonize.

This time, with less consideration than before, he was thrust back into the filthy cell. Early each day when he arose he felt much like a dirty monkey as he picked a morning average of more than fifty lice from his shirt. Meals were meager—twice a day one small rice ball and water. But providentially he was allowed one meal from the outside, which his friends brought him each day.

As the days, weeks, and months passed, his faith became ever stronger. Even without a bed of any kind, he slept well at night and, with the blessing of God, increased in weight during the seven months he was there. Just as for Peter, the prayers of the faithful ascended like incense before God.

Then the Adventist prisoners began to note a perceptible softening in the heart of the chief. One day he was heard to say, "If Christians are really to believe the Bible, certainly the Adventists are right."

Eventually, in recognition of his ability, Yamagata's release was ordered so that he could be used in an army college as a professor of physics. Japan was feeling keenly the shortage of scientists.

"But remember," he was strictly warned, "that if you keep your Sabbath you will be arrested again."

He made no comment. Reporting to the army college designated by the order, he found that because his release had been unaccountably delayed, another man had been hired already.

Once more there was rejoicing in the homes of the faithful that night. They knew that it would have been virtually impossible for him to keep Sabbath in the army school, where classes were held every day.

The authorities continued to keep Yamagata under close surveillance as he sought another job—one that would allow him to have at least two days off each week in order that he would not necessarily be checked for keeping Sabbath. This seemed also to be asking the impossible, for it was now toward the end of the war and everyone was supposed to be working seven days a week.

Again he was considered for army draft, for everyone who was not working specifically for the purpose of war was now subject to induction.

And then again in that fearful war God stepped in on behalf of Yamagata. It was one evening about five months after he was released from the Tokyo prison that he heard a knock on his door.

Such a knock could mean almost anything, and that anything usually tore at the heart.

But this time it was different. One of his friends who had been a fellow professor at Hosei University stood there in the *genkan* smiling.

"I have good news for you," his guest said, smiling and bowing the traditional bow of the cultured class.

Yamagata was still skeptical. He had seen such smiles before.

His friend continued, "They want you to teach mathematics and science at the technical college in Ibaraki Ken. You need to teach only two days during the week."

A big smile swept across the young professor's face. His family joined in audible expressions of gratitude and relief.

God had not only fulfilled the promises of Psalm 91, but had done it far beyond their fondest expectations. For the two-day job took Toshio

Yamagata and his family out to the country college, away from the city where bombs were soon to fall, and paid him a salary three times as great as that of the average professor for only two days' work a week.

Thus God had laid the foundation for the future of Japan's great Seventh-day Adventist educator. Those precious promises in *Thoughts from the Mount of Blessing* had been fulfilled.

"What wonderful blessings come from God," she told us cheerfully. "He has saved all of us!"

Imamura's Blessings

AMONG Adventists in Japan few names tug at the heartstrings so tenderly as Imamura. When the going is rough or friends seem apparently without gratitude, that name makes them embarrassed at their discouragement. For Imamura is the name of a family of heroes: Father, Mother, son, and daughters, who each in his own way has demonstrated twenty-four-carat, solid-gold loyalty to God.

This story centers around Shinobu, the only son of Pastor and Mrs. Masaichi Imamura. I tell it in this way because I have come to know him well and because the providence of God did not allow me the opportunity to know his faithful father.

It was on a midautumn day in 1934 that Shinobu's humble life began. That day, October 30, was of no special significance to the run-of-the-mill Japanese, but to the young Christian couple the fact that their first child was a son was extremely important. He was given to God in like manner as Simeon had dedicated the Babe of Bethlehem.

The war clouds were rising eastward in the Pacific some six years later when young Shinobu began his studies at the Fukuoka Shogakko—a Japanese elementary school.

The teachers could not help liking the smiling youngster, ever obedient and thoughtful, except for one problem: He would go to school only five days a week.

"Why did you miss school Saturday?" the sensei asked him after his third weekend absence in a row.

"I go to Sabbath school," was the forthright reply.

"The what?"

"The Sabbath school, Jesus' school," Shinobu answered in his childlike way, surprised that everyone didn't know about the Sabbath.

The matter was reported to the school principal, and the parents were called in.

Steadfast at a time when some of the other church members were weakening, the young pastor and his wife had nevertheless been caught in a difficult circumstance.

"How is it," Pastor Imamura was questioned, "that some of your church members send their children on the sixth day and you don't?"

It was difficult for the pastor to reply without reflecting on the guilty members and without evincing disloyalty to them. In Asian tradition he knew well he must take care not to cause any of his flock to lose face.

"In a matter like this, I suppose that every man must speak for himself," Pastor Imamura averred. "It is my deep conviction that the seventh day was made holy by God, and my conscience would not be clear if I permitted any member of my family to violate it." The young minister was breathing an earnest prayer to God that his testimony might be received favorably.

The principal, well aware of the work for the poor in the community that had been so efficiently accomplished by the pastor and his wife, warmed up as best as he could, without losing face himself.

"Do you have any suggestion?" he inquired sympathetically, but with some reserve.

"I wonder," Pastor Imamura replied, sensing the opening God had provided, "if it would be all right with you if my wife should teach the children on Sundays. She would also take special care that they do not fall back in their other studies here at your school."

"Let's try it," the principal agreed slowly. "But remember, much depends on you."

It was now December of 1941. The thunderheads of the Pacific had exploded into full-blown war. Anything Western had become suspect. And Christianity, no matter how Asian its origin, was definitely considered Western. The Japanese war code was as foreign to the teachings of Christ as were those exploding bombs to the tranquil lagoons of Honolulu that December 7 sunrise.

Strange visitors began to tramp up the second story stairs of the little Fukuoka church. Day by day the small parsonage downstairs became more and more the object of surveillance by these "visitors." Before long the veil of secretiveness was thrown off and the hobnailed boots of the dreaded thought police crunched up the soft wooden stairs that heretofore had been caressed only by reverent slippered feet.

"Mamma, what do they want?" Young Shinobu was frightened at the ill-hidden concern of his parents.

"Don't worry, son, just keep hold of the hand of Jesus," the young mother replied, patting his head with her left hand while holding closer to her bosom little three-year-old Junko.

There was indeed reason to be concerned, for in time of war all Japan was subject to the severest of national disciplines. Anyone who did not agree willingly and completely with every national order and policy was suspected of espionage.

"It is the children that worry me," the mother confided to her husband after they had tucked their two little ones under the heavy cotton *futon* one evening. She was thinking also of the one soon to come. This time of trouble brought the young couple close together in consecration and mutual encouragement.

"Okasan," the pastor addressed his wife endearingly one evening after the children were sleeping quietly on the *tatami* floor, "I want you to make me a promise."

"Yes? What?" The questioning reply came in a voice that revealed an understanding of more than was carried by his words.

"We have been warned several times now," he began.

"Yes," was the sober acknowledgment.

"And they may take me any time."

The pale mother nodded silently.

"You must not give in one inch, not on anything, no matter what they say or do to me," he broke out in a troubled river of words. "I want you to promise me that no matter what comes you will not lose your faith in our Saviour."

She nodded once more.

"Remember Psalm 91," he continued, fingering the pages of his well-worn Bible. "Remember too that 'there hath no temptation taken you but such as is common to man: but God . . . will with the temptation also make a way to escape, that ye may be able to bear it.' " He brushed back a stray lock from her forehead and patted her cheek. She looked up at him and smiled.

"I promise. With the help of God, I promise."

Shinobu tells what happened next:

"It was in 1943, September 20 to be exact, when early one morning we were awakened by the sound of heavy footsteps. I was only a third grader and do not remember much except that I was scared.

"A man had come into the house and was searching the *oshiire* [a Japanese closet] and was looking through Father's bookcases. The next thing I knew, Dad was taken away in a truck. I thought he might be going somewhere on a trip. I was so young that I really did not know what the police had come for.

" 'Good morning,' I had greeted them.

"'Good morning,' they had replied. And that was all.

"Mother was silent in her bravery. We had no idea what was going on, but could now tell that something was wrong.

" 'What is the matter, Mamma?' I asked her.

" 'Father has been arrested for his faith. We must pray.' So we prayed. 'Now you go on to school,' she instructed me.

"I went to school that day, and everything went as usual, as I remember. But when I returned, Father wasn't home.

" 'Where is Daddy?' we children asked that night at suppertime, sensing something different.

" 'Daddy has been taken to the police department and may not come home right away, maybe for quite a while,' Mother answered. She showed me the warrant. I couldn't read much. I remember only the expression on her face.

"I went to see my father once at the prison. He had his head shaved and looked very strange. When I first saw him he was sitting in a room, but when I came in he stood up. I don't remember what we talked about. The main thing was not words anyway, but just seeing him—just to be there with Dad for a few minutes.

" 'Good-by,' I said to him.

" 'Be good to Mother and sisters, my son,' and he smiled tenderly. 'Keep close to Jesus, keep very close.'

"They began giving us trouble about the Sabbath again at our school. Mother had come to the school every year to explain carefully about our religion and why we believed in the Sabbath. But now the teacher in my fourth year was a stern lady. Nevertheless she was a good instructor. I can remember well about two or three occasions when she showed what a good teacher she was.

"On the other hand, she had no sympathy for Christianity. Her prejudice seemed almost bitter.

" 'You will come to school on Saturday,' she warned me severely. And then she said some things that are better for me not to say. It was embarrassing to stand thus before the class; but she *was* a good teacher."

The punishment meted out to the boy before his class was multiplied by the Asian psychology of *memmoku*— public disgrace, or loss of face, which to the Japanese is sometimes worse than death.

As unrelenting as Shinobu was firm, she would send a messenger to his home each Sabbath morning with a note warning him to come to school and fulfill his "duty to our Emperor." Often she would pose embarrassing religious questions.

Looking out on a cloudy day, she would ask, "Where is Amaterasu Omikami?"

Shinobu knew well this Japanese sun god, but would not recognize the sun as god.

Rebuked again and again for not answering what was to him an impossible question, she would ask him about his relationship to the Emperor—questions "that were hard to answer sometimes." Sometimes his sister, Junko, was confronted with similar questions and embarrassing circumstances.

"Do not worry," their mother would comfort them when they came home at the close of the day. "God knows, and He will overrule." So it went through the war, with Mrs. Imamura working hard on Sunday to provide the two their sixth day of required studies—studies that are much more serious in Japan than in many nations, for the Rising Sun of the Orient has some of the highest and most rigid educational requirements in the world.

Shinobu continues the story:

"Mother would gather us around her every morning and every night. She always read us encouraging things from the Bible, and we sang songs together. She would recount all the blessings that God was giving us. Sometimes it seemed hard to find them, for we did not have much to eat. Besides, we were to feed Father too. He seemed to be slowly starving to death. When we would sometimes wonder why all these things were happening to us, Mother would read Hebrews 12:5, 6 or Revelation 3:19 to remind us that God was showing His love to us by refining us, by preparing us for heaven.

" 'Someday you will find that God has a special plan for you,' she would tell me lovingly, 'and this is all part of His plan.'

"I now realize that this was true, but some of the things were hard to understand in those days.

"August 2 of the next year, 1944, had been a weary day for Mother. She was working hard to keep us alive. It was a hot evening, and we were sitting around a little table for *yuhan* [a light evening meal] when somebody called Mother to the door.

"Returning soon, she said quickly, 'I am going to Father, so you pray for me.'

"We children were sleepy and went to bed. Several times during the night we would awaken, waiting for her to come home. Then about midnight we heard people's voices out in the *genkan* [the entrance to the house]. I went out to see what it was all about, and saw Mother, Grandfather, and Tsurumi San, a faithful church member and close neighbor of ours, with a stretcher there.

"It seemed as if Father was sort of sleeping.

" 'Daddy is home.' Excited, I woke up my sisters.

" 'But our daddy is sleeping in Jesus,' Mother tried to explain carefully. We did not really understand, except that we knew he had not had enough food to live.

"Mother was not well now either, but she was always brave. She was always counting her blessings.

" 'Surely Jesus must love us very much,' she would repeat."

Their father had been dead several months now, and the frail mother's strength was ebbing away as she worked ever harder to keep her little family together.

The war was now coming closer to Japan, and directly in its path on the southern island, Kyushu, was their city, Fukuoka. Air-raid sirens struck terror to the hearts of the people, who had been told that it was impossible that any American plane should come over their sacred land. Shinobu and his sisters had been fascinated the first time with the strangely wonderful pattern made by the great bombers.

Then one evening at dusk that curious sight and ominous sound again brought fear to the hearts of the Fukuokans. It was a fire raid done to perfection as the great planes moved in for a circular run about the city and then crisscrossed to make sure that there was no escape.

The Fukuoka church and the little parsonage went up in flames. "We ran from place to place," Shinobu recounts, "along with our neighbors with our *futon* ["bedclothes"] over our heads to keep from being burned. It was an experience I don't like to remember.

"Mother gathered us close around her some time later that night, and we had a little prayer meeting.

"What wonderful blessings come from our God,' she told us cheerfully. 'He has saved all of us!' It was true, for death was all around us. Compared with others, we were hardly knowing sorrow. We never had appreciated our God so much as we did that night after the bombing was over."

Soon that little mother was taken to a tuberculosis hospital. She is still there now—eleven years later. But she is improving, and, best of all, she is winning many hearts to Jesus.

Junko is doing well in the nursing school at the Tokyo Sanitarium and Hospital. And little sister, Kazuko, is studying earnestly at Japan Missionary College Academy.

"As for me, I know that God is with me," Imamura San noted in concluding his story—one that was drawn from him only after weeks of persuasion.

Such were Imamura's blessings.

As they gripped hands under the murky surface their hearts sang a duet of Christian love.

The Makings of Heroes

DURING World War II Japan had its share of men who had the stuff heroes are made of. Not all of these were youth, but all had early shown their metal.

There was Pastor Ogura, the earnest Adventist leader, who had found his faith as a youth while studying in England, and who had chosen to be cut off from his wealthy family rather than to give up his God. He it was who led the small Adventist mission during the war, after the Americans were gone, with much of his administration carried on from a lonesome cell in Tokyo Central Prison.

Then there was old Pastor Kuniya, the dean of Adventist workers, the first to be baptized in Japan, more than forty years before the war. Even in advanced age he took the abuse of the police and of his friends for refusing to bow to the Emperor.

Another aged couple were Pastor and Mrs. Fukazawa. Once a well-to-do family, they had given their lives to work for God. During the war their Rock of Gibraltar stand was a continuing inspiration to the Adventist church. The prison keepers knew them well.

Pastor Eikichi Seino, one of the most stalwart, dignified, and active pastors of Japan was given some of the cruelest treatment of all. In Fukuoka prison, even in advancing years, he would not consent to a passive religion to mollify his persecutors. He was active for God. Despite his age they stripped him naked in the icy hours of evening, kicked him, slapped him, and subjected him to indignities deserved by no man, much less a sensei of his mien, in a country where such humiliation is often considered worse than death.

The stories of Tsuruji Hasegawa and Kiyomitsu Hatada, though no more heroic than many others, nevertheless reveal with special clarity the binding influences of Christless religions, and how the Spirit of God moves on the hearts of Asian men.

Once a dedicated Confucianist, Hasegawa was nevertheless a seeker after truth. The more he examined himself, the more he was sure that by nature he was sinful.

"My deeds were all sinful," he recounted later. "I was surprised and I was ashamed and I began to be angry with myself." He had studied Confucianism because it advocated morality. "But Confucius didn't give power to live it," he had concluded. "I must find a truth with power."

A friend urged him to study Buddhism. So he went to talk seriously with a priest of a nearby temple.

"I understand that Buddhism teaches about hell and Paradise," the serious young student began.

"That is right," answered the yellow-robed priest.

"Do these places really exist? Are these realities?"

"Hardly," the priest smiled superciliously.

"Do you mean that such a thing is a lie?"

"Why, of course, if you want to call it that."

"Then why are you preaching the way of Buddha and why are you telling people lies?"

"Well, circumstances sometimes justify the means," he replied, eyes half closed.

"In other words, it is perfectly all right to tell a lie if it seems necessary?"

The priest shrugged his shoulders.

It was the earnestness of young Hasegawa that brought him to a Christian lecture, thence to a Bible study, next to a Protestant church, and finally to a lay Adventist pastor. It was this same earnestness that led him to quit his job for the Sabbath and that carried him, content in God, through his prison-cell days during Japan's great war with the West.

It was at Hakodate, the harbor city on the southern coast of the frigid northern Japanese island of Hakkaido, that Pastor Hasegawa was "interviewed" by the thought police.

"What is the matter with you?" he was queried, first sympathetically and then sternly. "All the other Adventists have given up!"

Hasegawa's face showed his disbelief of their challenge, but his heart fought loneliness of spirit. His prosecutor became especially bitter, using every device and diatribe his inventive mind could contrive.

"This is the last chance you will have to speak," he was finally warned. "In the prison where you are going, no prisoner talks to another."

With heart desolate except for his faith in God, the Adventist pastor walked the silent path to his gloomy cell, contemplating the possibility that his fellow believers had given in. Discipline was almost vicious in its strictness. Truly, communication of any kind between prisoners was prohibited. In the yard, at labor, and in the community bath, where conversation would normally have been the light of life, a morose and lonely cloud settled over most of the prisoners, many of them political offenders.

Then one day in the lineup Hasegawa was electrified. There, facing him in another line just across the yard, he thought he saw Pastor Kaneko.

"They haven't all given in!" he exulted silently, thanking God.

Identical thoughts raced through Kaneko's mind. He raised an eyebrow in recognition. Hasegawa cautiously lifted his brow in answer. They were brothers in Jesus! Heart warmly spoke to heart across the icy prison pavement.

They did not see each other again for a long time. Then one day by sheerest "coincidence" they met again, this time in the prison's community bath. Under the sharp eyes of calloused guards they dared not speak. But bit by bit Kaneko edged toward Hasegawa. Going down into the water for a soak so typical of Japanese bathing, Hasegawa somehow came up a little closer to his Adventist brother.

Repeating this several times, always wary of the alert eyes of the guard, Kaneko and Hasegawa finally went into the water together. As they gripped hands under the murky surface their hearts sang a duet of Christian love unheard in that somber, steamy room, but that echoed through the arches of the throne room of God.

"M-m-m," Pastor Hasegawa fellowshipped, out of the ken of the guard.

"M-m-m," answered Pastor Kaneko. And those slightest sounds, of no significance to another soul in that bath, spoke universes of comfort to the two heroes in the dreary months to come.

Pastor Hatada's story is best told in his own words:

"I was born in the country of Kagoshima in the southernmost part of Japan. My folks were earnest Buddhists belonging to the Jodo Shinshu, a sect of the west Honganji denomination."

Just as in Protestantism, there are a number of denominations and many sects in Buddhism.

"When I was little, together with my parents, I had to pay homage, sitting every day in front of our miniature family shrine. I was also taught the Buddhist scriptures in daily worship. That is the way they made strong Buddhists. I had to memorize many passages of the sutras, the Buddhist Bible. We recited them again and again.

"In our home were several miniature shrines and many household gods—war gods, the god of the rice fields, the water god, the fire god, the god of the mountain, and so on. I grew up among people who worshiped millions of gods. And I believed simply and completely in all of these gods until I was at least twenty-four years old.

"We were taught to be patriotic with all our hearts, and were certain that the Emperor was a living god.

"I am a short fellow, only five feet tall, and was especially willing to do anything for the Emperor to show my patriotism. So I was a special enemy of Christianity. That was my way of showing my patriotism. My prejudice was complete. In the neighborhood of my country home the people thought that if anyone listened to Christianity, he was in great danger; and if he ever believed in it, he would have his liver taken out while he was alive.

"I was sure that I would never need the Christian God. After all, we had plenty of gods of our own—eight million of them.

"The spring I was nineteen years old I left my home village for Osaka, Japan's second largest city, and one of the ten largest in the world. I was going to become somebody. I was filled with ambition and was determined not to go home again until I had become a successful businessman.

"So I went to work in the Kawakita Electric Company. I worked earnestly during the day and went to school every night, but finally I became sick and had to quit school and change my work.

"Next I went to work for a lumber company, where I could get more exercise, but after a while I became the treasurer of the company and was again doing seat work. Here again overwork and intemperance made me sick. White rice and poor food gave me stomach trouble and some heart disease, both of them caused by beriberi. Now I had to go home, and was disgraced because I had not realized my ambition.

"Still an earnest Buddhist, I began to think seriously as I lay sick.

" 'What will man become after death?' This was a serious question, especially after the doctor visited me one day.

" 'Am I not a good Buddhist?' I began to question myself. 'Why do I lose my patience? Why can't I be a little more noble? Why can't I live on a higher plane?' I was not at all satisfied.

"Determination seemed to help me get better, and soon I was working for a group called Kibosha, meaning 'hope,' whose aim was self-improvement. It was led by Seiko Goto, a man who had become famous for this kind of work. It was not a Christian group but seemed to have some Christian principles.

"My heart became stronger but my body was still weak.

" Why don't you go to the masseuse?' my friend suggested one day. I had not thought of that before.

" 'If you cannot go to her, she can come to you,' he added optimistically.

"A meeting was soon arranged, and the widow and her two children came to see me. I was soon impressed by her kind attitude toward her children and by the atmosphere of her presence wherever she went—by the way she met strangers, her meekness, her cheerfulness, her tender voice, and everything about her.

"She began to tell me the precious lessons about Jesus, her Saviour, and read to me from Matthew—the Sermon on the Mount. I was interested in such stories because they meant self-improvement.

" 'How do you live such an abundant life, such a happy life?' I asked her one day. 'I would like to know your secret.' I didn't know that she was a Christian. If I had known I wouldn't have asked such a question. As a matter of fact, if I had known she was a Christian, I wouldn't have asked her to give me treatments—my prejudice against Christianity was so keen.

"My question seemed rude, but I felt constrained to ask it again.

" 'How can you maintain such a consistently high level in your life? What is the source of your happiness?'

" 'It is because of my religion,' she answered.

" 'What kind of religion?'

" 'It is Christianity.'

"So that was it. I felt that I shouldn't have asked. But it was too late now.

" 'There are many kinds of Christianity,' she pointed out. 'Just like Buddhism, Christianity is divided into many sects, perhaps hundreds—many more than Buddhism.'

" 'What is the name of your sect?' I asked.

" 'My group is the Seventh-day Adventists, Kagoshima church,' she replied thoughtfully.

" 'That is quite a name,' I said; 'what does it mean?'

" 'It means that God made the heaven and earth in six days, Sunday to Friday, and rested on the seventh day, Saturday. This Sabbath is the memorial of His creation because God rested and made it holy. We are keeping that day.'

"She told me more and more—that the Old and New Testaments say that Jesus is coming back again and that 'Adventist' means that this is the church that believes Jesus is coming again.

"After hearing this I couldn't oppose her any more. After all, she had helped me and she had convinced me of Christianity by her own life. The wall of prejudice had broken down, and *I* was almost ready to accept anything.

" 'Here is something for you to read,' she offered before she left that day. 'Read it carefully.' She laid in my hands a Bible.

"That night I read the first verse in Genesis, 'In the beginning God created the heaven and the earth.' I believed it simply because it was the best thing I had ever read. I knew that the theory of evolution could not be true. Now it seemed as if that by believing in this one verse I was given so much light that every other question in my mind was solved, and for the first time I had great peace. It may be hard to understand, but in my rejoicing I soon regained my health.

"I followed this woman from place to place as she gave her Bible studies. First to the little town of Ichiki, then to a resort. I was hungry for the Bible. And finally she went to Kagoshima, where I was introduced to two fine men, Pastors Onoda and Ishibe.

"Mrs. Araki, a blind worker there, was especially kind to me.

"Because of the clean life these people lived, my faith became stronger. Example was their greatest teacher.

" 'This is it,' I finally said to myself one day, and made up my mind to follow Jesus completely. God had waited a long time for me, a sinful man. I was so thankful that I could not keep back my tears. At last I believed in Jesus Christ as my personal Saviour.

"I told my friends about it. 'You will lose your job,' they said. 'You are begging for trouble. Many bad things will happen to you. Remember your liver!'

"I wrote a letter to the president of the company in Osaka for which I had previously worked, telling him that while recuperating I had become a Christian, that God is the Creator and I would like to keep the Sabbath as a memorial of His creation.

" 'If you will give me the Sabbath off, I will be willing to work much harder on the other six days,' I wrote him.

No answer came.

I decided it was necessary to go to see him. Stopping at my home village, I talked about my conversion to my parents.

They were very unhappy.

" 'Poor Kiyomitsu San,' they grieved to each other. 'He was such a good boy, but poor Kiyomitsu San is going to have his liver taken out while he is alive.'

"Nevertheless I was now sure that there is no name under heaven except Jesus whereby we must be saved. So I was not afraid of any opposition or persecution.

"Going on to Osaka, I met the president of the electric company. God helped me, and when I talked to him about my religion he was understanding and kind.

" 'Man needs some kind of religion,' he encouraged. 'You keep your Sabbath.'

"I was deeply grateful.

" 'You just take good care of the other employees of our company,' he added.

"I worked earnestly for that company, and when the time came to pay tithe on my first salary, it was a joy I cannot forget. But trials came each time payday came on Sabbath. I had to get somebody else to do my work on that day, and I had to have the ledgers, papers, and cash all ready before the Sabbath. But God always helped me, even though I was not very healthy.

"Little by little Elder Seino, of the Osaka church, taught me to eat brown rice instead of polished rice and to eat more healthfully in other ways.

" 'The body is the temple of the Holy Ghost,' he told me, 'and therefore we must keep the spirit and the body in health.'

"On the very day Emperor Hirohito was led to the throne in his great coronation, I accepted my inheritance in the throne room of God and was baptized in Osaka's Yodo River."

Thus began the new life that led Kiyomitsu Hatada to consecrate himself as a worker for God. It led him through threats of death, through long periods of imprisonment, because he held his royal birth in the family of God of greater value than his being a subject of the earthly Emperor of the Land of the Rising Sun.

Earnestness in finding the truth of God and firmness in holding the standard high, we found, is the stuff of which heroes are made.

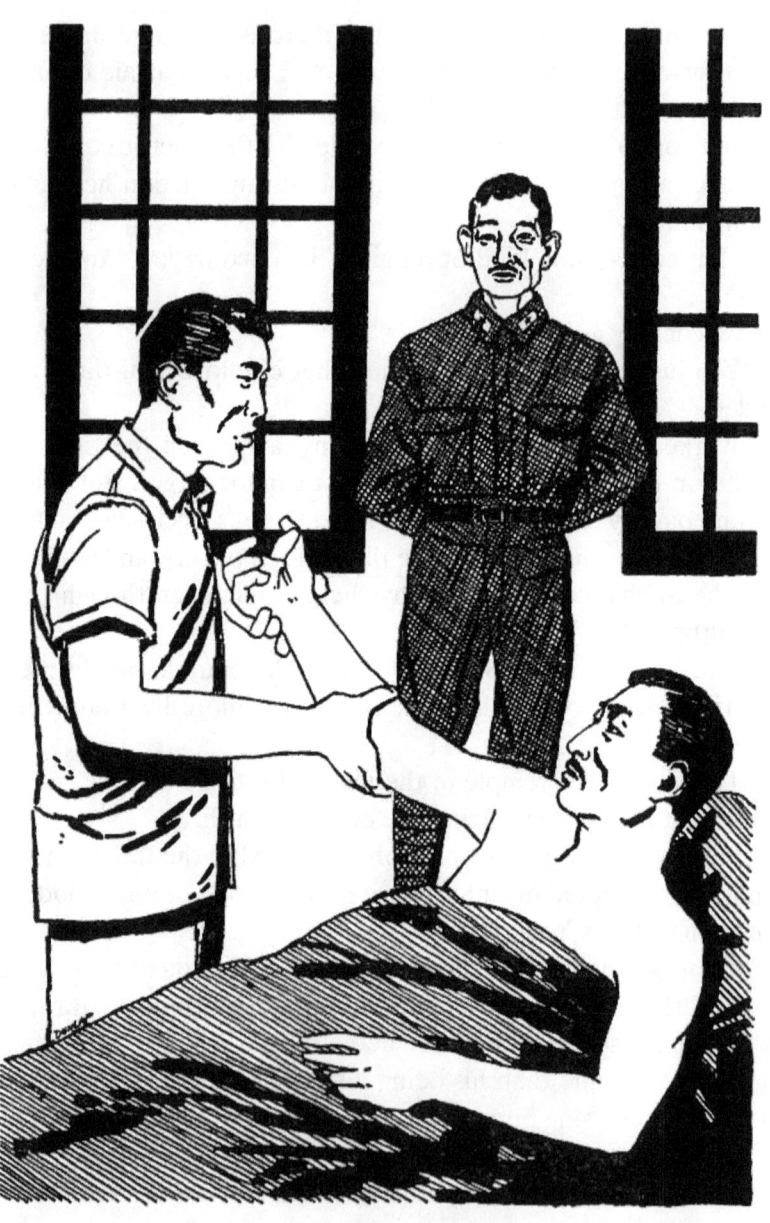

Yamamoto became the warden's official masseur, and, like Joseph, the favorite of the prison.

Yamamoto Finds a Daniel

"WITHOUT a doubt Toribiong is the Number One Palauan."

This seemed like an extravagant statement for such a responsible man as United Nations Administrator Herran to make. But this capable statesman was serious as he spoke to Pastor Kelstrom. He was aware that Toribiong was making plans to go to Japan Missionary College, but was asking for a temporary delay until the new government was well established.

"There is no leader so promising on Palau," he added, underscoring his assertion.

The story behind the rise of Toribiong, the modem Daniel who presides over the national congress of Palau, is a dramatic commentary on the ability of God to appropriate to His glory the devices of the enemy.

The success of God's plan for this key South Sea Island Adventist, strangely enough, hinged on the faithfulness of an obscure Japanese boy, the third son in a family of fourteen children.

The son of a farmer, Yamamoto San had been brought up in a poor but dedicated Buddhist home.

"We worshiped before Buddha morning and evening," he related later. "It was the first thing we did when we got up, and the last thing we did before going to bed. Even breakfast and supper were sermon hours. Father loved to talk about Buddha and his teachings. He never failed to travel far to attend the special spring and autumn services.

"But we were very poor, and the future was dim for us boys. We could not go to college. My elder brother worked at the village hall and I found a job at the post office.

"One day a friend stopped by the mail window.

" 'I was looking at your pictures the other day, Yamamoto,' he spoke earnestly. 'You ought to become an artist.'

"The idea excited me, but I wanted to make sure. So I consulted a fortuneteller.

" 'What do you want to be?' the seer asked me.

" 'I want to know if I should be an artist,' I answered uncertainly.

" 'Do you like to draw?'

" 'Yes, very much.'

"With that the fortuneteller arranged some *omikuji* in his hand. It was a Japanese way of drawing lots.

" 'Draw,' he invited, 'and may the gods be with you.'

"I drew, entirely naive about the methods of the unscrupulous old man.

" 'It is favorable,' the wizened old seer enthused. 'You must become an artist.'

"Without hesitation, and without too much judgment, I soon arranged an apprenticeship to a commercial artist. This man, however, was not faithful to his profession. He had so many other interests that I found my training to be unsatisfactory.

"Discouraged, I suggested to his foreman one day that I wanted to quit.

" 'I will show you a good place,' this man sympathized.

" 'When?'

" 'Tomorrow night. They are very good people. They are Christians, and you will be able to have one day off every week.'

"I was very happy at the prospect.

"Sure that I would easily resist Christianity, I answered him readily. 'Yes, tell him soon that I will work for him, that I will come right away.'

"When we arrived at the artist's house the master was away. But his wife was there, and I will never forget the first sweet smile as she came down the stairs with a small child in her arms.

" 'This is Yamamoto Seiichi,' my friend introduced me, putting my family name first as the Japanese always do.

"*'Yoku irasshai mashita,'* she welcomed me. Thus far everything was encouraging.

" 'Where do you live?' she inquired.

" 'I am from Yamaguchi Ken.'

" 'Why, I come from the same prefecture,' she said enthusiastically. 'Just where do you live?'

" 'Our home is at Iwata, in Tsuno County.'

" 'That is my home county too,' she exclaimed. 'Isn't this interesting?'

"This drew us closer, and through her kindness I was confident I could find work here.

"That night I stayed at my friend Shimoto's place. I can still remember the potato and *miso* [bean paste] soup. The kindness shown me greatly strengthened me, and I returned to the artist's shop. The master was there.

" 'Yamamoto,' I announced my name, Japanese style, bending deeply.

" 'Tabuchi,' the master introduced himself, bowing slightly in acknowledgment of my humble overture. 'I understand that you want to work here.'

" 'Yes, sir.'

"He looked me over thoroughly, but always with a sympathetic smile.

" 'We will give you a try. You will be a temporary worker. The rest is up to you.'

"Resigning my former job, I got my belongings together and moved to the Tabuchi home. But from the first it was plain that he was testing me.

" 'Your first job will be to wash these windows,' he ordered, 'and after that you will report to Mrs. Tabuchi.'

" 'Yes, sir,' I replied, still optimistic. From then on my work was to cook breakfast, clean the house, and take care of the children, one seven, one four, and the youngest, a year old.

"I was not learning art very fast, but somehow I was not worried about speed in learning the profession. For soon, without realizing it, I became deeply interested in the teachings of the Bible. Every morning and every evening we studied. Their love and their example momentarily disarmed me. Day by day my questions were answered. But down inside of me this new Christianity was fighting my old Buddhism. Often I would visit the neighborhood temple and listen to the Buddhist sermons while I was taking care of the children."

Yamamoto San had been with his new master for only a few weeks when his former employer called on the Tabuchis. In Japan it is a serious thing for one man to employ an apprentice away from another.

"I have come to take Yamamoto back with me," he told Mr. Tabuchi.

"I don't understand." The Christian artist was puzzled.

At this point Yamamoto San stepped into the conversation. "I didn't mean any personal offense in leaving you. I just left because you were not around to give me training."

The visitor became visibly disturbed.

"I left because there wasn't any hope at your place," the youth continued, stammering himself in deeper than ever.

This angered the questioner more.

"At least don't blame Mr. Tabuchi," Yamamoto pleaded.

At this point Tabuchi San took over the conversation. "If you still claim him as your apprentice, take him along," he offered.

"But I don't want to go back," the youth insisted, half defiantly.

The visitor turned away ominously. "I will be back," he promised.

"But he never returned to claim me," Yamamoto told us later.

"The Tabuchis taught me to pray, to pray to the true God. They taught me about the Sabbath. They introduced me to Pastor Kajiyama, whose gentle attitude and smiling face made a deep impression on my mind. It seemed that God was taking hold of my life.

"One day Pastor Kajiyama's sermon was on love. I remember that I was so impressed that I bought a present and went all the way back to my former employer's place to give it to his children and to apologize to him for my rudeness.

" 'Welcome, Yamamoto,' he greeted me, much to my surprise. He inquired on my progress.

" 'It was your fault,' his wife told her husband later as we sat around the *hibachi* [charcoal pot]. 'It was your fault that Yamamoto left. You hadn't done your duty as an artist.'

"I visited him many times after that and gave him literature.

"Pastor Kajiyama would come each week to the Tabuchi place early in the morning before breakfast to give Bible studies to his workers. It was because of this study and the encouragement of Pastors Andrew Nelson and Francis Millard that I began to think about going to Japan Missionary College. Then one day Pastor Hide Kuniya came to our town for an evangelistic effort.

" 'Would you like to be a worker?' he asked me in his fatherly way.

" 'How do you mean?' I had not thought about being a minister, but I surely wanted to go to school.

" 'I was just thinking that a young man like you should go to school and prepare himself for God.'

" 'I would very much like to go to school,' I assured him, and wondered whether this might be God's call.

" 'Have you taken your physical examination for the army yet?' he inquired.

" 'No, not yet.'

" 'Well, if it is God's will you may be going to school instead of into the army,' he encouraged, and then invited me to pray with him.

"I didn't realize what I was praying for that day when the physical examination did come. But I prayed anyway. 'God, let me be in your army instead.'

"There I was with many other young men I knew: Hayashi, Uemoto, Saito. Down the row of doctors they went. Every one of them passed Class A. Then the doctor in command came to me.

" 'You are Class C,' he advised briskly without explanation. I was well and hardy, and to this day do not have any idea why I was placed in Class C and exempted, except that this must have been God's plan.

"For seven years I studied for the ministry at Japan Missionary College, supporting myself by manual labor. Then my adventures began.

"From the college I was sent to Hiroshima in southern Honshu, and from there was sent as a missionary to Palau in the South Seas, to islands that were then territories of Japan.

"Almost immediately after the outbreak of war with America in December, all Christians were placed under deep suspicion. The police began to visit my meetings. Then one morning I was called to the door. There they were waiting for me.

" 'Yamamoto?'

" 'Yes?'

" 'Prepare to come with us.' Without formality I was quickly taken to jail.

" 'You are charged with action contrary to the interests of our nation,' the judge advised me in a trial that was private except for my guard.

" 'The Christian doctrine teaches against the permanent prosperity doctrine of the Emperor.' The tone of his voice was not harsh, and I knew that what he said was true.

" 'What is your answer?' he inquired courteously.

" 'I believe that what I am teaching is in the best interest of our nation,' I pointed out not too hopefully, and tried briefly to explain.

" 'I am very sorry.' The judge nodded to my guard, and I was taken away to my cell.

"But down in those islands, away from the Japanese mainland, I was treated much more charitably than many of our workers."

The rest of Yamamoto's story is told by his friends:

Even as he was walking through the prison gates he was preaching the coming of Jesus. The native policemen saw something different in this prisoner and treated him kindly. Yamamoto said that angels were always with him. The prison keepers soon began to give him more and more privileges. In Japanese prisons the warden is usually given wide latitude by the court.

Yamamoto had in the prewar years also learned well the art of deep massage, for in Japan the masseur is usually a well-employed man, and often a tradesman will thus pick up extra money during the evening hours. Now, having learned that the warden was suffering from rheumatism and wished a treatment, the new prisoner offered his services.

"Are you sure you can do it well?" his guard queried, somewhat skeptical, but anxious himself to have a part in a good turn for his chief.

"I am only offering to help him. Let *him* decide my skill."

"I will report to him at the next change of guard and will let you know."

The warden was delighted at the prospect of such relief, which he had thought was as far as Japan.

"Bring him to my quarters this evening at eight o'clock," he ordered enthusiastically.

After that Yamamoto became the warden's official masseur, and, like Joseph, became the favorite of the prison.

Sensing the favorable attitude of the warden, Yamamoto sent an informal message to him through the guard one day.

"May I worship with my friends on my Sabbath? I will honor your trust." An earnest prayer accompanied this request.

A reply came more promptly than Yamamoto had even anticipated. "You may worship with your friends, but of course you are prohibited from proselyting."

The warden instructed the guard that he was to go with Yamamoto to every meeting he attended. This meant Sabbath school, church, and cottage meetings. Day after day the native policeman guarded him, and Sabbath after Sabbath accompanied him to meetings with the believers. More and more he became impressed with Yamamoto's godly life in prison and out.

One day the policeman who had been *ordered* by the warden to go to Sabbath school and church every Sabbath spoke quietly to his prisoner.

"May I be baptized too?" he asked, like the eunuch of Ethiopia.

"Why, yes, if you believe in Jesus as your personal Saviour," Yamamoto San promised solemnly.

"I believe," came the same sweet answer that has echoed down from apostolic times.

That guard was Toribiong.

After the war the U.N. Trusteeship decided that the Palauans should have reasonable self-government and called for an election. Toribiong was voted by his community to represent them at the Palau Congress. Now an Adventist minister of deep consecration, he had done much to clean up the villages and elevate the moral standards of the people.

Meeting under the general direction of the United Nations administrator in a free election, the congressmen emphatically elected Toribiong president of the congress.

It was with good reason that United Nations Administrator Herran had spoken to Pastor Kelstrom. Toribiong, the man of God, was clearly the leader of his nation. Yamamoto, the Joseph of Palau prison, had in the providence of God found a Daniel.

The morning for the final assignment came. The men were all lined up in the strictest military manner.

God and the Gyoraitei

"*BANZAI! Banzai!*"

Nine slender highly trained young men shoe-spooned themselves into their sleek torpedo submarines.

"*Banzai! Banzai!*" Once more came the shouts from the men on the dock as the tenth, Commander Kondo, in his practiced way slipped himself in and closed his compartment over him.

These were the *gyoraitei,* the *kamikaze* of the sea— Japan's famous suicide submariners.

Attentive and expectant, alert for prearranged signals, nine pairs of eyes watched closely for the lights on Commander Kondo's boat. This was their last practice, their last night before sudden death, for on the morrow they would ram their torpedo subs into the cream of the attacking American fleet. They would die for the Emperor. They were to leave their inlet at Bo at the end of Satsuma Peninsula in southern Kyushu. Last-minute intelligence reports would tell them the rest.

These nine pilots were proud men. They were proud that they had been selected to die for their Emperor. They were proud to serve under so skilled a *gyoraitei* officer as Kondo. The blood flowed fast in their veins. They mopped the perspiration from their furrowed brows as they waited for the signal. It was an all-important night, for upon it depended the mission of the morrow. They must die gloriously!

Commander Kondo waited patiently, but ever alert to the radio transmitter at operational headquarters. He had learned well that the obedience of the *gyoraitei* pilot must be absolute. A gesture of impatience would not be tolerated for a second. Fingering the controls of his carefully machined little sixteen-foot torpedo sub, Kondo first contemplated his mission of the morrow. He was not entirely happy about it, for it meant that he would never see his sweetheart again, nor his mother. The *gyoraitei* pilots never came back. They must never come back.

His mind went quickly back through the years that had brought him to this appointment with destiny. Minds do strange things in times like that. He had been given more opportunity than many of the young Japanese men. Graduated from the commercial department of the Meiji University two years before, where he had been a leader in his class, he had looked forward to a promising career as a businessman in Japan's great industrial trust, the *Zaibatsu*.

But the war had changed all this. In urgent need of qualified officers, the war lords had cut short the university courses of study by six months. All students were compelled to enter one of the services. Kondo San had chosen the navy.

First, there had been a preliminary training period in the Manchurian fortress city of Ryojun. It had been a trying six months, but he had learned to do "anything for the Emperor." It was not long before he was marked as officer material and was selected for special training as a *gyoraitei* commander.

"I want you to understand clearly what you are being asked to do," his training captain had told them one day. "The *gyoraitei* is a torpedo bomb. It cannot come back, lest you disgrace His Imperial Majesty. You are destined for the great privilege of dying for the Emperor."

In early 1944 the men were shifted to Sasebo for this training. Missions were to begin immediately. Kondo's education had been effective. He was filled with the Japanese spirit and could hardly wait for the chance to fight.

The morning for the final assignment came. The men lined up in the strictest military manner.

"Unit one," the training commander barked out. "Nemoto, Fukushima, Ishibashi . . . ."

Kondo San listened carefully for his name.

"Unit two. Hara, Hayashi, Shibata . . . ."

Kondo San was straining more than ever for that all-important word.

"Training command," continued the commander briskly, "Yonemura, Kondo. . . ."

"Why? What is this? Why have I been selected for the training command?" Kondo thought to himself half embarrassed. He wanted action, but for some strange reason he had been selected as a training officer.

"You will proceed to Okinawa tomorrow." The orders were impersonal. There was no appeal.

The Japanese were now certain, from their intelligence reports, that the American Army would soon attack Okinawa. Their fears were soon confirmed.

Looking up into the limpid evening sky of the tropics, Kondo San watched the dreadfully beautiful pattern of the American bombers as they prepared for their runs. All had been ordered to the shelters, but as an officer he had certain prerogatives, and his curiosity overcame his need for safety. He was awed and angered by the great birds as they came in with chronometer timing from all points of the compass, meshed into a perfect bombing pattern, dropped their fearful cargoes, and were gone.

There were many raids by smaller planes, and often Kondo San and his men were taken by surprise. Danger dwelt with them like the air they breathed. Death surrounded him until it became more common than eating. But somehow the keen young Buddhist officer was saved time after miraculous time when shrapnel cut down those at his side.

One day Kondo was called in before the adjutant of his top commander.

"Kondo San."

"Yes, sir."

"You will be flown to Kanoya immediately." The young commander sensed his next assignment, for Kanoya was not far from the *gyoraitei* training base.

"You will proceed from there to Sasebo. Your orders await you there. They are urgent."

"Yes, sir." And with a salute Kondo San wheeled sharply and left.

The next day the American Army landed on Okinawa, and Kondo's former outfit was wiped out.

Learning of this a few days later, when he had arrived at his new post in southern Japan, Kondo was deeply impressed.

"I have need of you," a still small voice seemed to be troubling him. Was this the voice of his ancestors?

He felt even more impressed that he was being led by an unseen hand when he learned that same day that some of his men and all of his personal baggage had been destroyed when their boat was sunk en route to Sasebo.

With his usual meticulous care Commander Kondo polished the remainder of his unit, timing them to the second. The nine youths did not realize the seriousness of their situation as their young commander did. He knew that if anything were to be saved now, desperate action had to be taken. Yes, it would be a great privilege to die for the Emperor.

In staff meeting one morning a few weeks later, the fleet commander was outlining the schedule of attack. First he turned to young Kondo.

"We are expecting an attack from the American fleet tomorrow night. They must not reach this base."

"Yes, sir," Kondo affirmed as his fellow officers nodded in agreement.

"Our intelligence tells us that they will be about fifty to seventy-five miles south-southwest of Bo by dusk."

"Yes, sir." The youthful commander was looking his superior straight in the eye.

"You will lead your unit to intercept them according to plan four. Much depends on you because our air support is grounded from airfield damage."

"Yes, sir."

"For the Emperor."

"Yes, sir."

"Banzai," the officers agreed in unison.

Now the ten keen young pilots were making their final check for their date with death. A thousand thoughts seemed to be flooding Kondo's mind as he pressed his earphone against his head lest he should lose an all-important word.

"Unit three," the radio crackled. This was it, Kondo was sure.

"Three over," was the snappy reply.

"Unit three! Commander Kondo!" His earphone literally rattled.

"This is Kondo, unit three," came the tense answer.

"Mission delayed."

The young commander hadn't realized how tense he had been until he again stood before his captain. Gripping his hands at his side, he tried hard to control his nerves and to hide his disappointment.

"Emergency word from Tokyo," was all the captain said.

"Yes, sir."

"Turn in, Kondo."

The young commander obediently headed for his barracks. The next day the war was over.

Once more, even in bitterness, Kondo was feeling the presence of an unseen hand in his life. But where should he go now? There was no organized veterans' program, educational plan, or even orderly disbandment of the Japanese Army. Here he was with nine intelligent young Okinawans on his hands and nowhere to turn, nor anything to eat. They could not return to Okinawa, for it was no longer Japanese territory. And they must take special care lest they invite the suspicion of the occupying forces. They had no land, so they could not raise food. There seemed to be only one possibility—the sea.

So they became fishermen.

Working carefully together as a team, they would fish and then trade their catch for rice. Indeed, they worked so closely that soon they were suspected by the American Army of being subversive. And one day toward the last of 1945 Kondo San was arrested. Newspapers reported his condition as top news, "GYORAITEI OFFICER GOES TO KAGOSHIMA PRISON."

In a humble home not far away an Adventist preacher was studying his Bible one evening by uncertain light. A gentle knock easily shook the sliding doors.

Pastor Takagi moved across his *tatami* floor, slipped on his *zori,* and, stepping down into the *genkan,* he cautiously pushed back the door.

"I am Takahashi," the visitor bowed deeply. *"Shibaraku de gozaimasu* ["It has been a long time"]."

"Dozo," the pastor invited, returning his visitor's bow and motioning him inside. Soon Takagi recognized his guest as Takahashi, a son of one of his former church members at Nagoya.

"I have come to see you about my friend," the newcomer began, without going through the usual Japanese *aisatsu* [the complicated formal greetings that are almost invariably used on such occasions].

"I am glad you have come."

"It is about my close friend, Kondo San. I know you are busy, but I want you to visit him."

"Where?"

"He is in Kagoshima Prison, and none of us ordinary Japanese can go there. But we have been thinking that maybe a Christian minister can obtain the favor of the American soldiers."

"I would very much like to help, but— —" Takagi San

hesitated. His heart said to help, his mind said to be careful lest he be implicated in anything that might damage his church.

"God will help you," urged Takahashi.

"Yes, God will help."

Takagi gingerly made arrangements to visit the young prisoner. His disappointment was compounded when, after all of his efforts to secure a pass, he found Kondo reluctant to see him.

"I am a Buddhist. I was born a Buddhist. Why should I see a Christian minister?" he earnestly told his patient visitor. It was clear that he was still filled with the Japanese spirit.

"I understand well," the pastor sympathized.

"I am a student of Buddha," Kondo continued. "I will find truth in him."

Takagi San's heart was drawn out to the young man whose spiritual imprisonment was even worse than his confinement of body.

"I will try to help you get out of here," the pastor promised. "I will try to have an understanding with the army."

There was something about the tenderness and patience and earnestness of Pastor Takagi that impressed Kondo San.

Week by week the pastor visited the prison. Week by week Kondo's confidence grew in the Christian leader. Love again was finding a way. Finally, in late 1946, the Occupation Army, too, demonstrated its confidence in the Christian pastor by releasing the prisoner in his care.

As they studied the Bible together one day, Kondo San turned to Takagi across the table at his left. "Pastor," he spoke steadily, "I believe now I am beginning to understand the strange feelings I had many times during the war, feelings of certainty that a powerful hand was directing me wherever I went."

"Yes, how true."

"God saved my life not a few times, Sensei."

Teacher and student, they studied together day after day and week after week even after Kondo was stricken with pleurisy. Before long he married his sweetheart, who joined Takagi's Bible studies. But once again fortune seemed to turn its back on the talented youth. For three years and a half he was stricken with tuberculosis, unable even to move from his bed. The doctors gave him up to die.

"God will see me through," he voiced confidently when the doctors finally gave him up. And, true to his faith, the strange Hand that had guided the young torpedo submariner through a thousand dangers, lifted him from death's bed, helped him become an earnest worker for the truth. At his side his faithful wife, in the providence of God, has become a leading worker in the church schools of the nation.

Every five minutes they shot flare balls into the air, and we had to dive under to keep from being shot.

From the Shadow of the Gallows to the Shadow of the Cross

THE husky youth stood with right arm upraised. But he was more heard than seen in the dim light of the village hall. Nearly the entire populace of the farming village shivered before him as the *kita kaze* (Japan's winter wind) whistled around the thin walls of the village hall and vied with the village rats to find its way through the open places under the eaves of the heavy straw roof. Every inch of the *tatami* (straw mat floor) was crowded with silent Japanese figures.

This youth was a convicted murderer. He had struck terror to the hearts of men. Violence had been his friend.

But the outward chill of this night could not overcome an inward warmth that was reaching the hearts of those village people on that snowy night in 1954. Those central Japanese farmers were not being cowed by a desperate and skillful killer. They were being pointed heavenward by a son of God, a converted man whose big smile and warm heart seemed to reach right around and take them into the confidence of one who has begun to know his Saviour and his Lord.

The powerful youth had been born to the poorest of families in an Okinawa village in April, 1925, the first son in his family. Desperate for even the most meager sustenance, his father was finally driven from Okinawa to Saipan to seek a livelihood for his growing family.

In the Orient the first-born son is not only honored but is also held to responsibility. So when Saburo Arakaki's father headed for the far-off central Pacific island, leaving behind his wife and four children, Saburo was charged to "take care of Mother and the children for me and for your ancestors."

But the eight-year-old child could not cope with the problems that were soon to arrive. His hard-working mother soon became discouraged. Assuming that her husband would not return to her, and uninhibited by Christian standards, she divorced him and married another.

Saburo tells the story from there on.

"After that we four children lived with our old grandmother. Our mother did not see us any more, so our lives became harder than ever. The situation was soon so serious that I was sold for money when I was eight years old.

"Hearing of this some time later, my father called me to Saipan, and somehow I was able to gain my freedom. I don't remember exactly how. On Saipan I went immediately to primary school, but since my father had not remarried I was also his cook and laundryman. I did this for about five years. After that my father called my younger sister to Saipan for cooking and washing, and I had the freedom to finish my schooling.

" 'What do you want to be?' my father asked me one day in a thoughtful, fatherly way.

" 'I don't know,' was the only answer I could give him. Actually I felt that I had really lost my way. I was completely confused in my living thus far.

" 'Why don't you try the agricultural school?'

" 'Can I do that?'

" 'Yes, you have a good head, and I want you to have the education I couldn't have,' was his kind answer.

"In 1942 I took the agricultural examination. Fortunately, I passed it. Those were the days of World War II. Japan and America were now fighting fiercely. And from the start of my schooling I was taught strict militarism and the strongest patriotism. Every day we students learned intricate drills to build up our Japanese spirit. When we were promoted to the second year we began to do projects for the army, such as making airfields. We studied earnestly two hours a day, and the rest of the time we spent in labor, an average of eight hours a day, working like slaves.

"But it was a great privilege to do this for our Emperor-god, and by doing such work we were highly trained.

"About the middle of June, 1944, the Americans began to attack Saipan in great military force. Fighter planes flew over us. Warships boomed from the distance. It was clear from the beginning that America was controlling the island with its air and sea power. What were twenty thousand Japanese military men against all this might?

"On the day of that first attack all the students of our agricultural school went back to their homes. All, that is, except me. I was anxious to fight for the Emperor, and volunteered for the army to fight this enemy, which we had been told was so treacherous.

"But since I was only 18 years old, the captain would not let me go to the front. He asked me to work with the medical soldiers. Therefore I carried food and water for the wounded, sometimes taking them all the way to the field hospital. Other times, however, I had the great privilege of carrying ammunition to the battlefield. My daily duties thrilled me. My heart burned against the Americans. I was really hating them. I did not like the democratic way, and I was ready to die for my Emperor and country. That was the greatest honor a Japanese youth could have. So I was not afraid of anything. My every action was really adventure. My education had been so effective that even the soldiers were surprised by my work.

"During fighting I saw many miserable things—like the man who had just lost a leg and arm, trying to walk with one leg; the man who was newly blinded; the wounded child weeping in a cave beside his dead mother; and broken soldiers and civilians writhing on the wayside. Then there was the man who had committed suicide with a hand grenade, and the family that in desperation jumped over the cliff and into the sea. I learned that that was *yamatodamashii*—the Japanese spirit, which prefers death in honor to their beloved country and Emperor rather than to be caught by the fearful enemy.

"But the strong spirit that had been built up in me was not without bitter experiences. Much of those first twenty days we had neither food to eat nor water to drink. Most of what energy we had came from scattered stands of sugar cane. So we had much stomach trouble and suffered both physically and mentally.

"Finally we were pushed by the American soldiers to the northern extremity of the island—the place of our last stand. That final night all the survivors were given the order by the commander in chief to make a last attack. I wanted to join in the bold gesture and made ready.

" 'Don't go,' one of my sergeants warned me.

" 'Why?'

" 'Stay here and see what happens,' he warned.

"So I took refuge in a cave, and waited."

" 'Our fleet is coming!' the good news was echoed that Japan's combined fleet was sailing toward Saipan.

" "*Banzai*,' we returned one to another in muffled shouts. How happy we were, and what hope and strength that news brought to us. But if we did not move from the place where we were hiding, it was going to be dangerous by the next morning because the American fighters were drawing near. So we planned our retreat to Takocho Mountain about two miles away. This mountain had long been in our plan as the biggest and safest place.

"When the night came we began to take action. Some survivors tried to break through the American formation. But some of us decided that the safest way to go was through the sea. There was no other way, for we were trapped.

"So when darkness came, about forty of us renewed our vows to our Emperor and started off down the steep cliff to the sea. Into the rough waves we jumped and began to swim toward our destination.

"The water was cold and some places were deep. Fortunately, some were shallow. But the night was very dark, lighted only by the stars, which that night seemed cold and, fortunately, remote. Light was the last thing we wanted.

"But there was enough of it, as our eyes opened wide, to see dead bodies floating here and there. We discovered that we were swimming about three hundred yards away from land.

"And then trouble began for us. The Americans had discovered that some of us were escaping by way of the ocean. About every five minutes they shot flare balls into the air, so every time they were shining we had to dive down into the water and stay under, or we would be shot.

"But at that time I was not swimming alone. One of my arms was partly wrapped around my comrade, a heavy fellow who was badly wounded. His right arm had been shattered by a shell fragment before we jumped into the sea. It was this arm that I pulled on, asking him to swim as best he could with his left arm. But he relied more and more on me, and by the time we were halfway there he was almost dead.

"Soon when I called his name he did not answer. And yet I kept on pulling him. I was very, very tired, for we had not had much to eat the few days before. And when we came to the deep places high waves would hit my face. One of these hit so hard that it separated me from him.

" 'Have I lost him?' He was my friend, and I loved him very much. I threw my legs all around to find him, but I could not touch his body. I called his name again, but he did not answer. I tried desperately once more, but he was nowhere to be found.

"Finally it was plain to me that he was gone. Tired, and with my life in danger too, I gave him up and swam forward desperately.

"We swam almost all night.

"We dreaded that dawn, for we knew that as soon as the Americans could see us they would shoot at us, and that is what they did. We could not do anything to them. But we kept on swimming and finally arrived safely at a little beach.

"It was now dawn, and we could see our mountain sanctuary only dimly in the far distance.

" 'But we must somehow get there for refuge,' we agreed wearily. So as we carefully looked around we went forward, and in about twenty minutes reached the jungle at the foot of the mountain.

"Cutting our way through the jungle, we encountered wounded soldiers here and there. But we were too tired to do anything for anybody by then. We just wanted some safety, and finally we found a place we thought would be safe. We decided to stay there until night. Cold, wet, and hungry, yet with nothing to eat or drink, there was nothing else to do but go to sleep.

"With our clothes soaked with wet itchy salt water, our sleep was fitful, and our stomachs growled, our tongues searched for saliva, and before the day was over a new fear came into our hearts. We could see American soldiers on the high hill just in front of our mountain. They were looking carefully and systematically for Japanese soldiers. And once in a while just for a change, it seemed, they would shoot the machine gun blindly into our mountain. But it seemed that they still did not see us.

"When evening came we began to plan as to how we were going to take action, to find the safest possible course under these austere circumstances. Because of my long experience on the island I was chosen as the guide. I knew the topography of that area very well, so started out with some certainty.

"About seven o'clock, well after dark, we began to take action. I was marching at the head. It was dark, very dark. I could not see well in front of me. We were marching in the combination of jungle and cliffs—precipitous mountainside and root-tangled jungle. There was no road. We had to make our own. Only one who has cut his way through a tropical jungle can understand an experience like that. We walked, cut, stumbled, tripped, climbed, but always kept on and on.

"Finally we came out to a sugar-cane field, where there were a few wire lines staked alongside. We jumped over them easily without knowing what they were for. But the minute after we jumped, the American soldiers began to fire toward us fiercely. We all scattered.

"I do not know whether any were killed because I ran blindly, just ran and ran, without looking back. Soon I reached the left side of the jungle and found that one man was following me. I do not know what happened to the rest of them. But this other man and I began to walk forward into the jungle. We did not know where we were walking. We just roamed around in the jungle. We had not eaten or drunk anything since the day before, so we were hungry and thirsty. We tramped and cut our way through until finally we came out of the big tangled roots and leaves again.

"We were watching very carefully, and, fortunately, we had come to a trench. But there were no American soldiers this time. There we found plenty of leftover K rations—the cans contained biscuit and candies and cigarettes. There were also some cans of stew and potatoes and meat.

" 'Bikkuri shimashita.' We were certainly surprised. Our happiness could not be expressed in words. In the snugness of that trench we ate as much food as we could. After we had eaten plenty, we felt as if we were alive again. Then we put into our bags all we could carry.

"Our energy restored and spirit renewed by the food, we started again toward our destination. From then on we often found K rations, so we did not worry about food. Our stomachs were always full. And what is better than a full stomach at a time like this?

"But we were ever watchful because we did not know when we would run into American soldiers. Soon we met other Japanese, and again I became the guide. I did not like this job, but these were my orders.

"Traveling ever so carefully, we nevertheless again ran into an enemy formation. They were everywhere! The sentry discovered us and shot at us. But, fortunately, nobody was hurt. We changed directions and went forward toward our destination.

"Though we met the enemy on the way to Takacho Mountain five different times, we finally reached the top of the mountain safely. It took us two days. There we found more than three thousand soldiers and civilians. It was a big mountain and seemed like a safe place, hard for the enemy to attack.

"It was really a sight to us. Here they were eating rice and Japanese canned food, which they had found in caves that the Japanese Army had prepared before the fighting broke out. There were many such food caves in this mountain. So we also went to get some rice. And from that day on we had rice every day. We made our dwelling place in a tent. Others lived in caves and others in deep bushes. Some were in the holes in the cliffs. Some were in the holes of the rocks and others were hiding in the sugar-cane fields.

"Water was the big problem. There was not much water on this mountain and all were competing for it. Sometimes we took rain water from the trees or tent. Without our usual baths and with clothes becoming more and more dirty, our sanitation problem became serious. The lice flourished even in the seams of our pants and shirts. Some of the refugees had skin diseases, and some had other problems.

"But somehow the louse was our friend. The days were long ones, and it was hard for us to spend twenty-four hours. So we killed time by catching lice. That is how they helped us. The rest of the time we spent scratching, for when the lice bite, the skin becomes itchy.

"We cooked our food only at night, for if the Americans had seen smoke in the daytime they would have found us immediately, so quietness in the daytime was the order of the day.

"The American soldiers began to hunt us more skillfully than before. Nearly every day they were coming onto the mountain.

"'*Dete koi,*' they would say, meaning 'come out.'

" 'If you come out with your hands up, we will not shoot you,' they shouted through their interpreters.

"By now they were even watching for us at night, when we would go to get water or food. Lying in wait one night about thirty yards away, they fired their machine guns. Many of our fellow soldiers were killed. Many times that happened, but I was always saved.

"Those days they called me 'lucky.' Today I know that there was a different reason.

"One day somehow I was separated from a group of snipers I was guiding. The next day that group was completely wiped out. Another time about the middle of my year and a half of sniper life some Negro soldiers came into our hiding place. They had followed our footprints. It was about eight o'clock in the morning, and they found us sleeping. We had no idea that they had come into the jungle, so nobody was on watch. One Negro shot me through my jaw. The scar is still there. But there was nothing serious.

"Nevertheless we were always worried and anxious, for if someone did get hurt we had no medicine—none, that is, except the hand grenade. Those were days when men's hearts were cold. Men's hearts were worse than animals' hearts. The hand grenade seemed really the best medicine all right.

"Nine months later our rice ran out, and in desperation we planned to attack the American camp or its storehouse to find food. It was a risk, but we had to take it.

"Our first venture was at night, and fortunately we were successful. We stole a lot of flour and rice, bringing back as much as we could carry. We never went to the same place twice, for if we had they would have been waiting to shoot us. For two weeks we did this each night. But by that time every American storehouse was strictly guarded and each sniper who went stealing was killed.

"Finally we were forced again to the American dump. Here we found plenty of both food and clothing—many canned things, and sometimes bread, meat, candy, and cigarettes. And in the field and the jungle we found wild potatoes and papayas, the tropical food that so often supported our lives.

"But the Americans became even more difficult, and food harder and harder to get. Sometimes they would surround our mountain hideout for as long as three days at a time so that we could not even move. They would broadcast to us through the loud-speaker.

" 'Come out,' they would say, 'come out. We won't mistreat you. We will guarantee your life, so come out.'

" 'Yes, let's go,' we would mock. *'Ikimasho'* became a sad joke for us. We had been taught that death was much better than torture at the hands of 'American barbarians.'

" 'We have a nice camp for you,' they would urge again and again. 'There are many of your fellow soldiers waiting. Come on out.'

"But we did not believe what they said. We thought it was just propaganda. We had been certain that Japan would never be defeated in war and that war was still on, although now one by one some of our comrades did go out and surrender.

"Then about August 8, 1945, our latest cave was discovered by the Americans, who threw in tear gas. We thought we were being poisoned.

" 'This must be the terrible poison gas we have heard about,' we agreed fearfully. We endured it about ten minutes, but after that could not stand it any more. One of our group ran out first. He decided to surrender, but outside he found no Americans. Apparently they were just going from cave to cave and throwing in the gas.

" 'No Americans here,' our buddy said. 'Come out, everybody.'

"We all ran out. What if they did shoot us. We had faced death so many times and were so hungry that we were now becoming careless. As time passed our fellow soldiers became fewer and fewer. When the war was over in September there were only about two hundred snipers left. Among them there were a few civilians, of whom I was one. They treated me as an important man because I knew the topography of the island. So wherever they wanted to go they always asked me to lead.

"The food situation finally became so bad that we were eating snails and tapioca. When we cooked the snails we first broke the shell and took out the stomach. We kept the head part. After that we put it into the can, and stirred it with a stick. While it was being stirred, sticky water came out. Then we would boil it and, after boiling it, wash it with water a few times and make a stew or whatever we wanted. But some of us didn't get used to it, and we had bad stomach trouble. Anyhow, I tried to eat anything. We cooked in a one-gallon can we found in the dump. Our life was just like that of Robinson Crusoe.

"It was now late September, 1945, and the American soldiers were making plans for a big sniper hunt. They were surrounding our mountain so that we could not escape. We must prepare to fight even though we had only a little ammunition. Therefore, we determined to wait without making any noise—wait to let them shoot first and then we would shoot.

"But we were not in peace. We were now only 150 and were very much afraid. We waited and waited for them to come into the jungle, but they did not come. About one o'clock one afternoon they began to shoot mortar shells into our mountain. Somehow they had found out that there were still a number of snipers in the mountain. The shells fell in every direction. So furiously they came that we could not even move. They exploded all about us like a child throwing a handful of rocks on a nest of ants.

"Two hours this continued. Finally I got up from the ground and looked around. It was the first look I had had in more than an hour—a long, long hour. All around us the trees were down and there was a heavy cloud of smoke. Then as the cloud rose I shivered at the sight of many dead bodies about me. Even worse were the wounded soldiers crying for help.

"I was miserable and felt that I could not stay in this mountain any longer. We must move. With my friend Mr. Tsuchiya, a Japanese military policeman, I decided to attempt an escape.

"Tsuchiya San was a famous man in the mountain. He had gone to the detention camp many, many times. In fact almost twice a week. He knew all about conditions and always brought back good news. He always made us happy and encouraged us, although later we found out that nearly all of his news was false. That night three of us moved to a cave about a mile away.

"We admired Tsuchiya San. We thought him a very wise man, a capable leader, so we trusted him completely. We were sure he knew everything about the Japanese Army. The Japanese spirit burned inside him. After talking to him I decided again to die with him for the Emperor.

"After we had lived in the cave for a few days, half starving, the Americans again surrounded our mountain. We would watch our fellow soldiers going down one by one with hands upraised.

"But my heart, still burning with the Japanese spirit, would not surrender. I would stay to the end.

"But one night an old man came to our cave from the American camp. I thought he was a spy because he was sent by the Americans, and I wanted to kill him because he talked about how well the Americans treated the Japanese. Tsuchiya San, the military policeman, advised me to go anyway.

" 'You are a civilian,' he reminded me, 'and there are many civilians in that camp. They will treat you well.'

" 'I will not go,' I refused stubbornly. 'I will stay and die with you.'

" 'My ears are closed to you,' he said indifferently and would not listen. This was the same as an order to surrender, so I did. The next morning the old man and I went down the mountain, leaving everything I had. I felt lonesome without the few precious things I had saved.

"When we came to the crossroad the old man lifted his hands up and waved his handkerchief toward the Americans. In five minutes a jeep appeared in front of us with one white man and two Negroes. They jumped out, searched me, and motioned me into the jeep. I felt queer sitting there between the two Negroes. It was the first time I had seen either a Negro or a white man. But one of them gave me a cigarette, and then I began to trust them.

"At the detention office they asked me all kinds of questions about myself and the mountain, then placed me over in the civilian camp, well separated from the prisoner-of-war (POW) camp for the soldiers."

"It was now October, 1945, more than a year and a half since the Americans had attacked the island. Life in the camp was easy and the treatment was good. We had three good meals a day, and they trusted us and let us go outside. I was assigned to the quartermaster and handled food all day. But I was so used to stealing that I would steal and eat all kinds of food, and what food I didn't eat I damaged as much as I could, because I still hated the Americans. I still had the *yamatodamashii* spirit.

"One week later an unexpected guest arrived at our camp. He was Tsuchiya. As a soldier he should have gone to the prisoner-of-war camp, but somehow had deceived his questioners. He had been used to cheating men, and it was not hard for him to skillfully lie to investigators. I decided to protect him as a civilian, and right away introduced him to friends whom I trusted. They said they would help me protect him.

"Although he was a Japanese we changed his name into Okinawan and called him Tsuha San. We managed to work together and always made trouble. We were not satisfied if we weren't making trouble. Tsuha soon became a hero among our friends because almost every night he talked to us about the Emperor and taught us nothing but militarism. So by his teaching the Japanese spirit began to burn again in our hearts.

"We organized a secret group and made him the leader. Our purpose was to be alert to America and to anyone who spoke anything good about America. We hated anyone who did not have the Japanese spirit.

"We acted only at night. Sometimes we would make our way stealthily around the camp and throw anonymous letters to men and women who did not act like Japanese or who associated with the Americans. Sometimes we gave them punishment.

"The camp became afraid of us although they did not know just who was doing these things.

"One of these friends of the Americans was a Japanese news reporter. It seemed to us that he was always doing just what the Americans said. Actually he was doing the right thing, but we did not like him. Tsuha San had demanded that the reporter quit his job, but he would not do it.

" 'You must kill him,' Tsuha ordered me one night. I had a funny feeling in my stomach. Then I remembered the *yamatodamashii*. I resolved to do anything for the Emperor.

"So two nights later about twelve o'clock I went to his house to kill. But there was a child sleeping by him so I could not kill him then. I went back to Tsuha San and told him a lie.

" 'He is not at home,' I told him.

" 'We will kill him next time,' Tsuha answered stoically.

"I am glad now that 'next time' never came.

"Every chance I had, though, I acted like a madman. I called out men and women who acted pro-American and beat them. I loved my country and my Emperor-god. My heart was burning. I was twenty years old and could not think good but could do anything evil.

"After about a month in camp Tsuha San again ordered me to kill a man whom the people did not like.

" 'He is a traitor,' Tsuha declared angrily. 'He has talked bad about the Emperor and about Tojo. He has told us news that is not good news. And wherever he goes he acts like an American, dresses like one. He is a working supervisor, and he treats some prisoners roughly.'

"When I received this order from Tsuha San I was happy. My hands were tingling, for the Japanese spirit was burning in my heart. My knife blade was sharp. I talked about it to my two best friends who were in our group, and they wanted to help me, so I let them. These two friends had no parents and sisters so they did not care what happened to them. They were desperate. They didn't care if they died. One night we gathered together and talked over plans. Tsuha taught us how to do the job. With my American bayonet and revolver I felt very brave. I was not afraid of anything.

"That night about nine o'clock I reconnoitered the place, and three hours later I sneaked into his house, where he was sitting Japanese style on the floor.

" Who is it?' he asked. Who is it?'

"He was never allowed to hear the answer.

"I very quickly hurried back to my quarters and went to bed. But I did not feel well. I was worried. I shook Tsuha.

" We followed your orders,' I told him proudly.

" '*Arigato,*' he thanked me briefly and went back to sleep.

"I went back to bed, but all sleep left me. I kept hearing footsteps and voices outside. Sure enough, the people already knew what had happened. They were walking to and fro.

"The next morning I saw people gathered here and there talking about the case. They did not know who had done it, but thought that the murderer had already left the camp and escaped to the mountains. All were happy though because the traitor had died, and that made me happy and proud. The American military police and the native policemen lost no time investigating the case. They called everyone in the camp for investigation and finally put two native detectives to search out the offender. All of us were investigated, but I was not suspected because I was so young.

"But soon the camp began to feel the pressure. Privileges were taken away. The U.S. watches and rings that were in the hands of the prisoners were confiscated. Some of the Japanese soldiers in the civilian camp were caught and sent to the POW camp. People began to complain against the man who had killed the traitor.

"The pressure became more and more severe, and soon we decided that we must leave. If we did, we reasoned, the attention would be diverted to us and the military police would assume that the murderers had escaped. So we decided to become Japanese snipers again, and left. Sure enough, the people in the camp began to live freely again.

"But we were back up in the old mountain.

"The American Military Police officers sent a Japanese agent to our mountain to invite us back to the camp and to reassure us. We had been given advance notice of his arrival through our friends in the camp.

" 'He is a spy for America,' we agreed.

" 'Arakaki San, you will kill him,' Tsuha ordered, handing me an American revolver with brief instruction on how to use it in this case. He carefully supervised the whole thing.

"After that I was not afraid to kill him. I was not afraid of anything.

"It was late November, 1945. The Americans were dropping handbills here and there broadcasting that the war was over. We did not believe this, but Captain Oba, the Japanese military commander, sent Tsuha down near the American headquarters to check for sure. He went down and brought back with him Major Ito and some newspapers and magazines.

"That night we gathered closely around him and heard the true but sad news that the war was over. The soldiers cried with agonizing tears. I could not cry, but I did not feel good, for all our fighting and suffering had been in vain, and now our burning Japanese spirit was fading away.

" 'You will all surrender on the first of December,' Captain Oba ordered.

" 'But what about *us?*' three of us asked, aware of our civilian status.

" 'We will disguise you as real soldiers so that you will go to the POW camp instead of with the civilians, and you will be safe.'

"There was nothing else to do, so we did as we were told. About eight o'clock in the morning, December 1, 1945, fifty-two of us surrendered. Again we were disarmed, investigated, and sent off on work detail.

"One morning about nine o'clock, when we were cutting grass around the stockade, a Military Police jeep drove up swiftly and unexpectedly, and stopped suddenly in front of us. My heart fell as I recognized the two detectives and the Military Police officers who had questioned us in the civilian camp. My heart was beating fast and I thought of running away, for something made me feel that they would find us. Looking around for a chance, all I could see were Military Police rifles pointing at us and machine guns aimed at us from the tower guards. The Military Police blew a whistle for fall-in, and we lined up in two lines. One by one they investigated, and before long Tsuha and I were caught.

"We were removed quickly to the civilian prison and placed in the hands of the native police, who hated us so much. They did not like the Japanese because during the war the Japanese Government had treated them like slaves. And now they were ready for revenge. The American Military Police left everything in their hands.

"As we were being transported to the prison Tsuha moved over toward me cautiously.

" 'Don't confess anything,' he ordered in an undertone; 'don't tell them a thing.'

" 'Don't worry,' I reassured him, still kindled with the old Japanese fire.

"The interrogation by the native police began. Tsuchiya—they knew his name was not Tsuha—was the first man to be called, and I soon followed.

"They started firing questions at me so fast that I was

" 'What is your name?'

" 'Yamada,' I lied.

" 'I said, "What is your name?" '

" 'Yamada.'

" 'Where did you come from?'

" 'I am a Japanese soldier.'

" 'If you are a soldier, then why did you attempt to escape from the camp?'

"No answer.

" 'Who killed the two men? The one in the camp and the other in the mountain?'

" 'I don't know anything,' I lied again.

" 'We know your name, and we know who you are. Come now, Arakaki. Tell us why you escaped from the camp.'

" 'Because of the news that the Japanese fleet was coming near to Saipan,' I answered, collecting my thoughts.

" 'You lie,' they challenged. 'You know you lie.'

"They tried their best to make me confess, but failing, they threw me into the lock cell until the next morning. The quizzing started all over again, but still I did not confess.

"In the evening it happened all over again, until finally they got so mad that they told me they were going to torture me.

" 'Go ahead and do what you like,' I answered, bluffing.

"They took me into the prison kitchen and laid me down on a large table. Seven of them were there, and each took hold of my hands and feet so that I could not move. One man then got up on the table with a water hose and forced it into my mouth. They turned the water on full force and tortured me with the water until my stomach bloated and the water came out of my nose and ears.

"I got mad and struggled and kicked the man who was holding the hose and he fell down on the floor. This made them all the more angry. They began to beat me with sticks until I became unconscious. The next morning I woke up in my cell suffering and groaning. Soon I heard a small voice in the next room through a tiny hole. It was Tsuchiya.

" 'Confess everything, Arakaki San. Confess everything.'

"I did not answer him. I could not understand.

" 'Tell them you killed the two men by yourself. Nobody gave you the orders.'

" 'And what are you going to do?' I asked incredulously.

" 'I am going to confess that I was sending the news, food, and some clothing to the snipers in the mountain. If I confess that, I will surely die with you. Let us die together. There is no hope for us to live since our country has lost the war.'

"I believed him and decided to confess.

"That night about ten o'clock, with other tortures all prepared, they brought me in for their questioning, but before they had a chance to do anything I confessed all that I had done. I confessed all, that is, except that I killed the two men by the order of Tsuchiya and the others who had assisted me.

" 'Who worked with you?' the policemen demanded.

" 'I did it by myself.'

" 'No, you didn't,' they countered.

" 'I tell you I did it by myself.'

" 'Can you show us the evidence?'

" 'Yes, I'll show you.' And with a flashlight we walked over to the camp latrine where I had thrown the bayonet, and later the revolver too.

"That settled the case as far as they were concerned, and from that night on the camp became quiet.

"Four months later, on the first of April, 1946, my trial began by military court-martial. The trial was a solemn one from the beginning. My two American lawyers and my interpreter could not fight much for me, for there was not much they could do. The trial had continued for just one week when I was sentenced to death. There was no alternative. There was nothing I could say. And why should I for I was determined to die with Tsuchiya for my country.

"After the trial my lawyer comforted me with words of kindness, but there was not much comfort in the words of anyone those days. For from that day on I began my prison life, waiting for execution.

"As I sat in my cell I kept wondering what was going to happen to Tsuchiya and when his case would be brought to trial. But it never came. Before long he was released and sent to a POW camp. Just before he left he came to my cell to say

" 'Don't worry, Arakaki San, they will never hang you. They will commute your sentence. Then I will do my best to work on your case. So don't worry. Take your courage. When you come out of prison, I will make your life easy. I will prepare a house for you and will prepare for your future wife. I will do anything for you, so be patient until the end.'

"But these words did not sound like the words of a man who expected to die with me for his country. His words did not give me any satisfaction or hope, and I began to realize that he was cheating me. I could not trust him any more.

"This made my suffering more intense than ever. In my heart I was hating him. I felt strongly that I wanted to tell all about him. I wanted to tell that he was the one who gave me the order to kill, for I had not been a killer before.

" 'What shall I do?' I was fighting inside, really suffering, suffering as I cannot describe to any man. But that old Japanese spirit came back and I determined that I would take the responsibility for the crime, be manly and die like a Japanese for my Emperor-god and my country.

"During the next year I did not know what to do. Sometimes I was so much in despair that I made up my mind I would commit suicide or break from the prison. But then I would think of my sisters and brothers or my fiancée. And then I would want to live.

"But all this time that dreaded death sentence hung over my head. I was despondent—could rely on nothing. Nobody was there to console or encourage me. The natives around me did not help the atmosphere of the prison either, for they hated the Japanese.

"One day a United States Navy officer came to me. Looking at me with a smile, he said, 'Arakaki San, we are taking you to Guam by ship tomorrow, so prepare to leave.' I was elated when I heard this because I thought, 'Soon I will be back to Okinawa or Japan.'

"But the war-criminal prison on Guam turned out to be worse than the one on Saipan. The regulations were stricter and the treatment was not so good. This was a real prison. Again my spirits began to falter.

"But six months later I had another visitor.

" 'Arakaki San,' the officer smiled, 'your sentence has been commuted to life.' The interpreter shared his happiness.

"I was so overjoyed that I did not know what to do. But with his next sentence my joy changed to sorrow.

" 'You will be sent to a prison on Hawaii.'

"I was glad to have my death sentence commuted to life, but to be sent to Hawaii made me again despair. I wanted to go to Okinawa, not to American territory. To me this disgrace was worse than death.

"On the Navy cargo ship I was treated well, in fact was not even distinguished from the others on the ship. They gave me the same food they ate, and even the crew were good to me. But I was suspicious of this treatment, and it did not change my attitude toward America.

"When I first was taken to the Oahu Prison in Honolulu I was determined not to learn English. I hated America and wanted to keep on hating her. Some of the inmates tried to be friendly with me, but their spirit and my spirit were entirely different. It was hard for me to get along with anybody. Sometimes when they tried to talk with me I became angry with them and fought with them.

"But I was worrying always. 'Here I am, young,' I thought; 'must I stay in prison all my life?' My commutation to life sentence had made me hungry for still a lesser sentence. I wanted to go home, but there seemed to be no hope. Nobody came to see me. I was always lonesome. No one would even write to me. I seemed to be cut off from everything.

"But then in the depths of my worry some little voice seemed to talk to me.

" 'Why don't you be a man? Lift yourself up and be patient,' it said. 'You are not going to get anywhere acting the way you are.' Even with all of my troubles this made sense to me and I determined to work hard.

"Before long the warden of the prison and the guards and the supervisors began trusting me. I became less suspicious and hard. They gave me a good job on the farm, and then promoted me step by step until finally I became an agent of the supervisor—the highest prisoner rank. This in turn made me all the more determined to be on good behavior. I made up my mind to be the model prisoner of the great Oahu Prison.

"About three years after the prison doors were locked behind me, an American-Japanese became my good friend. He could speak a little Japanese, and he was always kind to me. He would be my interpreter. And when he got something he would always share it with me. He was always studying a Bible lesson—the Voice of Prophecy. He wanted me to study it too.

"At first I refused to take it because it was written in English and I did not understand it. Besides, I did not like Christianity. We had been taught in school that Christianity was bad, for it did not respect our ancestors—did not agree with our spirit worship. But he kept on urging me, and finally I unwillingly began to study it just to make him happy, because he had been so good to me. My heart was beginning to learn the lessons of kindness.

"But I was studying without any purpose, and it took much patience from my inmate friend to teach me the answers to the Bible course questions. Then the little voice came to me again.

" 'As long as you are studying, you might as well get all you can get out of it,' it seemed to say.

"That made sense to me, and pretty soon I could hardly wait for the new lessons to come from the Voice of Prophecy office. I studied more and more earnestly, and by the time I had come to Lesson No. 10 I was studying like a hungry man. I was beginning to understand the truth, and the more I understood the more I believed.

"One day when I was nearly finished with my course a member of the Honolulu Japanese church came to see me. His name was Okuda, a kind and sympathetic man who asked me many questions about my experiences. I told him the whole story.

" 'Arakaki San,' he told me kindly, 'confess all your sins to Jesus Christ, and He will forgive you and save you completely, no matter what happens to you here.'

"I was very much impressed with his kind words and his earnest prayers. In my heart I determined that I wanted to be like him.

"Okuda San promised me that he would come to see me every week, and he always did. Soon he gave me a Bible for my very own, and before long my day did not seem complete until I had studied the Bible carefully. I especially liked 1 John 1:9, and confessed all my sins from my heart.

"Now prison life began to be different. I was sure that I had a personal Saviour and that I was changed by His grace. I now had a hope. I was sure, too, just as I had read in 2 Corinthians 5:17, that if any man be in Christ he is a new creature.

"By now my hatred for the Americans was all gone. The months were passing rapidly. I was happy about everything, everything that is, except one.

"It was the Sabbath. There seemed to be another little voice talking to me now, and I could tell it was the voice of Satan.

" 'If you do not work on Saturday,' it said, 'the warden and your supervisor will not trust you any more. They will think you have become a lazy man, and by and by you will not be released from the prison. You will stay in the prison until you die.'

"I did not know what to do. I felt as if I was committing the unpardonable sin.

" 'Arakaki San, are you keeping the Sabbath?' It was Okuda San who was asking me the straight question one day.

" 'No,' I answered frankly, 'I am not.' And I told him why.

"He explained to me how important it is that we honor God first, how great and powerful our God is, and how the Sabbath is a memorial of His creation. Then he prayed with me, with tears.

"I now determined, come what may, that I would go to the warden.

" 'Sir,' I said to him that day through my interpreter, 'I want to keep the Sabbath holy. I cannot work on Saturday.'

" 'I want you to be a Christian, Arakaki San,' he said with a big smile. 'You may have your Sabbath off.' He had understood almost before I asked. How, I don't exactly know, except for God.

"I was more overjoyed than ever before. The inmates nicknamed me 'Sabbath,' but even that did not bother me now. And on April 3, 1949, by special arrangements with the prison authorities I was baptized by Pastor Miyake of the Honolulu Japanese church. From that day on, my heart was completely lost in Jesus. The Japanese spirit had lost its war.

"Before long by the grace of the living God I had more than a hundred inmates who were taking the Bible course. And every Sabbath we conducted the Sabbath meetings with the help of the brothers from the Honolulu churches. God gave me four years to work like this for my friends in the prison. And the more we did it the more the warden and the supervisors and the guards came to trust me.

"Finally the warden himself began to work on my case to try to commute my sentence. He worked hard, but the first time he appeared for me he was turned down. But he was not easily discouraged, and the second time he obtained a reduced sentence, from life to fifty-four years.

"The third time he appeared for me it was reduced to twenty-four years. I thanked God for His great grace and prayed hard day after day, promising that if He ever released me from that prison I would be His earnest worker for the gospel. But if it were not His will, I would work right there in prison for Him.

"Then one day there was a fourth appeal. This time the Spirit of God moved on the heart of the governor of Hawaii to commute my sentence even further."

"Two months after the fourth appeal was made, and five years after I was baptized, I was called one day into the office of the warden, who was now my good friend.

" 'Arakaki San, I have good news for you.'

"Great hope welled up in my heart.

" 'On May 3,' he continued, 'you will be released from this prison.'

"I was so happy my ears were ringing. What a strange and wonderful thing to hear after all those years.

" 'The United States Navy will fly you to Japan, where you have been entrusted to the custody of the president of Japan Missionary College.'

"I could not say anything, not a thing. All I could do was to shake and shake the warden's hand with both of my hands. I'm sure I made him hurt. And right away I turned around and went down to the basement, which was my secret prayer place, and offered to God my thanksgiving prayer with happy tears.

"Yes, God saved me out of the prison. May 3, 1954, was a happy and significant day in my life. About eight o'clock that morning I walked out of the prison doors a free man. But greater than freedom from prison was my freedom in Christ Jesus. I must never lose Him, never lose Him."

The husky young man, face no longer lined with the worries of the condemned, but shining with the light of God, was pointing his hand heavenward before those Japanese farmers seated on the *tatami* floor.

"I have a living Saviour," he was saying to them; "won't you let Him be your Saviour too?" And Japanese men and women bowed their heads in wonder at a God that, unlike Buddha, knows how to love.

And so they will listen wherever Arakaki San goes. For from his theology course at Japan Missionary College he hopes to return to his native Okinawa, and thence to his foster home, Saipan, and the islands of the South Seas. But there his adventures will be greater, for he is now led, not by the spirit of old Japan, but by the omnipotent hand of God.

TEACH Services, Inc.
P U B L I S H I N G

We invite you to view the complete
selection of titles we publish at:
www.TEACHServices.com

We encourage you to write us
with your thoughts about this,
or any other book we publish at:
info@TEACHServices.com

TEACH Services' titles may be purchased in
bulk quantities for educational, fund-raising,
business, or promotional use.
bulksales@TEACHServices.com

Finally, if you are interested in seeing
your own book in print, please contact us at:
publishing@TEACHServices.com

We are happy to review your manuscript at no charge.

www.ingramcontent.com/pod-product-compliance
Lightning Source LLC
Chambersburg PA
CBHW070540170426
43200CB00011B/2491